AMAZING MISTAKES

Published by
Arcturus Publishing Limited
for Bookmart Limited
Registered Number 2372865
Trading as Bookmart Limited
Desford Road
Enderby
Leicester
LE19 4AD

This edition published 2003

ISBN 1-84193-176-4

Text design: Elizabeth Healey
Jacket design: Adam Renvoize

Printed in India

AMAZING MISTAKES

Michael Johnstone

Capella

CONTENTS

MYSTERIES

INTRODUCTION

The Collins English Dictionary defines 'mistake' as 'an error or blunder in action, opinion or judgement'. It would take a book many times the size of this one to chronicle the errors and blunders that have been made in thought, word and deed throughout history.

History is littered with mistakes – from Eve and her bite from the Apple of Temptation (her tenancy of the Garden of Eden was terminated on the spot as a result), to those who have sincerely come to believe that the world will end on a specific date, only to see dawn rise on the following morning.

There are mistakes that are trivial and have little impact on the way of the world. Take the sixteenth-century Scotsman who, inspired by those pioneers of early flight Daedalus and Icarus, believed that if he glued enough feathers to his arms and jumped of a high tower he would fly down to earth. Big mistake! He crashed to the ground below and was lucky to survive with just a few broken ribs and a lot of bruises. He did acknowledge a mistake: the feathers he used had been plucked from barnyard hens and chickens and everyone knows that these birds can't fly. He should, he said (when he came round) have used eagle feathers. History does no record whether or not he tried another flight of fancy.

There are mistakes that might appear to be trivial and irritating in one circumstance but disastrous in another. A badly closed door in a house may let in a draught, that's all. But a carelessly sealed hold on a passenger aircraft can result in tragedy – as happened when such a mistake caused a jumbo jet to crash a few miles north of Paris with the death of more than 300 passengers.

There are also mistakes that are amusing, such as that made by the poor typesetter who omitted the vital word, 'not' from one of the Ten Commandments. The result was that some pious Bible readers were told that committing adultery was not only acceptable it was obligatory.

And there are mistakes that are embarrassing. For example, when a rather vague publisher asked the small, familiar-looking woman he found himself talking to at a launch party what her husband did for a living. 'Oh, he's still the Duke of Edinburgh!' came the reply from Her Majesty, Queen Elizabeth II.

It would be a mistake to claim that this is THE definitive book on blunders. But there are examples of all sorts of them – some funny, others tragic; some famous, others less well-known ones; no matter, they all share a common thread. They were events never meant to happen, beliefs that we now know are completely unfounded or wrong, words never meant to have been said (or heard), or perhaps spoken but wrongly attributed. They are all mistakes.

C2000BC

SOMEWHERE OVER THE AEGEAN SEA

Flying High

When King Minos of Crete decided to build a labyrinth in which to imprison the terrible Minotaur – half man and half bull – he called on the services of famous inventor Daedalus to design it and oversee its construction.

Daedalus, assisted by his son Icarus, did a splendid job but later fell out with Minos, and father and son found themselves imprisoned atop one of Crete's highest mountains from which there could be no escape.

But Minos had reckoned without Daedalus's legendary powers of invention. The old sage and his son set about collecting feathers from the birds with which they shared their mountain-top prison. When they had enough feathers, Daedalus stuck them together with candle wax to make two pairs of wings – one for himself and one for Icarus.

The two strapped the wings to their arms and took to the air, but not before Daedalus warned Icarus not to fly too close to the Sun. Father and son set off and it wasn't long before they had cleared Crete and were winging their way over the Aegean Sea, aiming for Sicily. The younger man began to enjoy himself so much,

Feather-brained: *Icarus discovers the melting propensity of wax*

swooping through the sky like a swallow in summer, that he decided to see how high he could fly. Ignoring his father's warning, he flew up and up, closer and closer to the Sun.

Too late, he realized why Daedalus had warned him, for as the Sun's heat slowly melted the wax the feathers came loose and dropped off. With his wings falling apart, Icarus plunged into the sea and drowned. His heart-broken father flew on alone to Sicily where, it is said, he lived to a ripe old age.

Icarus's body was later washed up on a Greek island, which is now called Icari in his memory.

C1200BC

TROY

Backing the wrong horse

Inside the Horse: *what a really, really stupid plan*

Helen, wife of King Menelaus of Sparta, was said to be the most beautiful woman in the world. All she had to do was cast a glance at a man and he would fall in love with her. According to the Greek historian Homer, one of the men so smitten was Paris, prince of Troy.

One day when Menelaus was away from Sparta, Paris abducted Helen and sailed with her back to Troy. When the king found out what had happened, he was understandably furious and vowed to bring his wife back to Sparta. He persuaded his brother, Agamemnon, King of Mycenae, to combine their two armies, sail to Troy and force Paris to return Helen. The fleet that set sail under Agamemnon's command was reportedly one of the largest ever assembled.

The army besieged Paris in his fortress city of Troy, but he refused to surrender Helen to his enemies. One day at first light, ten years later, the Trojans were astonished to see that the Greek ships had sailed from the harbour. Paris and his men were obviously relieved that the long siege was over, but one thing puzzled them. Why had the Greeks left a huge wooden horse, standing not far from the city gates?

Suspecting trickery, Paris told his men to leave it where it was, but shortly afterwards a young man approached. His name was Sinon, and he had, he said, deserted from the Greek army, preferring to stay in Troy than face the long, tedious voyage back to Greece. He told the listening Trojans that the horse was a gift to them – a homage to their fortitude in withstanding the siege for a decade. The horse, he went on, had been dedicated to the goddess Athena and would protect their city.

Paris ordered that the huge horse be dragged into the city, where it became the focal point of celebrations that went on all day and late into the night. Only one Trojan, Laocoon, continued to be suspicious, but the people ignored his warnings and carried on carousing.

That night, as the celebrations continued, the Greek ships sailed back into the harbour under cover of darkness. The soldiers disembarked and made their way soundlessly to the city gates. Inside, the revelries had reached such a point that no one noticed Sinon creep up to the horse and open a door in its belly. Unnoticed, several Greeks dropped out and ran to open the gates. Greek soldiers stormed into the city, put its people to the sword and once they had reclaimed Helen, torched every building in the place.

The Trojans made the mistake of listening to Sinon. Had they left the horse where it was, the city may have survived into the present day rather than have passed into legend.

The story ends just as tragically for Menelaus. Among those who set sail from Greece was his son, Ulysses (or Odysseus), who had the idea for the Wooden Horse in the first place.

When the young hero set out, Menelaus told him that if the siege was successful and he survived the battle, to set white sails when his ship approached Sparta. This would give the king time to arrange a hero's welcome for his son. But if Ulysses died in action, his sailors were to be ordered to set black sails.

Sadly, Ulysses forgot his promise, and the ship's masts were sporting black sails when it approached its home port. In the mistaken belief that his son had died, the grief-stricken Menelaus threw himself into the sea and drowned.

Fact or fiction? Who knows! One thing we do know is that in 1870, the German archaeologist Heinrich Schliemann discovered the ruins of an ancient city on the Turkish coast at Husarlik. Subsequent excavations revealed that the city had been destroyed by fire around 1200BC, which fits with Homer's chronology of events.

8TH CENTURY BC

ANCIENT GREECE

Death of a strong man

Milo of Croton was the strongest man in Ancient Greece – and it was his very strength that caused him to make the mistake that cost him his life.

Milo hailed from the southern Italian city of Croton, a Greek colony founded in the 8th century BC by settlers from Achaea. He was a man of diverse interests and attainments. He was a skilled soldier and singer, a favourite of Pythagoras the famous philosopher/mathematician, and was himself the author of a book on science and natural history. All this, and his most famous attribute, his strength, is recorded in the writings of Plutarch, Strabo and other eminent historians of the ancient world.

Milo won the wrestling championships at each of the six Olympic Games held between 540 and 516 BC – the only man in the history of the ancient Olympics (776 BC – AD 393) to win so many victories. His strength was legendary throughout Greece. On one occasion he enclosed a ripe pomegranate in his fists and challenged his fellow athletes to wrest it from his grip. They tried their best: they failed. And when Milo finally opened his fist, there was not even the suspicion of a bruise on the fruit.

He performed his best known feat on the opening day of the games he dominated. He strode into the stadium carrying a fully grown ox weighing more than a ton on his shoulders and then proceeded to stroll across the playing field as if he was carrying nothing.

But sadly his confidence in his strength led to his downfall. Walking alone in the wilderness one day, he chanced across a tree, the trunk of which was partially split. Never one to dismiss a challenge, he must have decided to try to rip the two parts asunder. And that was his mistake. Somehow he became hopelessly entangled in the tree and with no one to help him was unable to free himself.

They found his body, partially eaten by wolves, a day or two later.

AD62

ANCIENT CHINA

Man overboard!

The Chinese poet Li Po met his sad end as the result of a mistake of his own making. Best known for his twin themes of wine and love, Li Po overindulged in the former one night when he was on a boat and was so enamoured of the reflection of the Moon on the water that, declaring he was in love with it, he leaned over to kiss it. Unfortunately, he lost his balance, fell overboard and drowned.

1245

PARIS

Perfectly imperfect

The general structure of Paris's Notre Dame Cathedral was completed in 1245. It was extensively restored between 1845 and 1864 but much of the original Gothic building survives. Anyone looking at it might assume that the men who built it went to extraordinary lengths to ensure that it was as perfect as it could be. They would be wrong. Notre Dame and many other Gothic churches have a slight kink in their main axes so that the nave lines up exactly with the centre of the altar. Some experts think that these kinks are the result of a simple miscalculation on the part of their architects. But it is more than likely that they built in the kink intentionally as an expression of humility and a reminder that only God is perfect. Such a deliberate imperfection is also seen in Persian carpets. Their weavers make sure that there is a slight flaw in the symmetry of the design as a reminder of humankind's imperfections.

Notre Dame: *perfect imperfection*

1492

SPAIN

Go west, young man

Very few people have heard of Cristobal Colon. He was born in Genoa, in northern Italy in1451. His father was a woolcomber and intended that young Cristobal would follow him in this occupation. But as he grew, the youngster began to have other ideas. Genoa was (and still is) the major port on the Ligurian coast. There's little doubt that he would often sit by the harbour watching galleys sail off into the Mediterranean, heading eventually for the East to load their holds with valuable spices. As he watched the ships' sails fill with wind, his head was no doubt filled with dreams of the adventures and wealth that a life before the mast could bring.

When he was fourteen, he persuaded his father to let him go to sea. By the time he was twenty he had made many voyages. One of the ships on which he sailed was attacked by pirates off the Tunisian coast. And around 1420 he was shipwrecked in a fight off Cape St Vincent and paddled his way ashore on a plank of wood.

In Portugal, he met and married Filippa Moniz, and it is here he probably took the name by which he is known to history – Christopher Columbus.

This was a time when more

and more people were beginning to believe what a few people had long advocated: the world was not flat, but round. Columbus was one such man. As early as 1474, he had conceived the idea that India and the Spice islands, which lie to the east of Europe, could, if the world was round, be reached by sailing west.

Encouraged in this belief by an Italian astronomer called Toscanelli, whose observations of the night sky had convinced him that the world was round, Columbus undertook several voyages into the Atlantic. On one, he sailed past Iceland. On another, he reached the Cape Verde Islands and the coast of Sierra Leone. More and more convinced that he was right, but lacking the money to fund a long expedition himself, he began to search for a sponsor.

First he approached King John II of Portugal, but the king was one of those who believed that the world was flat and told Columbus that he would hardly back an expedition that would end with ships sailing over the edge of the world.

Next, Columbus wrote to Henry VII of England, but the monarch who had only seized the throne from Richard III a few years before was more concerned with establishing his Tudor dynasty and bringing the finances of England into proper order than investing in such a risky venture.

Columbus then wrote to the powerful Duke of Medina Celi who suggested that he write to Isabella of Castille. Isabella and her husband Ferdinand referred the matter to their advisors, who at first turned the matter down, then reconsidered. After years of having his hopes raised then dashed,

Isabella and Ferdinand eventually agreed to sponsor Columbus's voyage.

On August 3, 1492, Columbus set sail on the *Santa Maria* with 50 men, attended by two smaller ships, the *Nina* and the *Pinta*, with another 70 men aboard.

Even by the time the small flotilla reached the Canary Islands, some of the men were voicing serious doubts about the wisdom of carrying on. Columbus, deaf to their concerns, pressed on. Days turned into weeks. The weeks into one month, then two, by which time the crew were on the point of mutiny.

Then on Friday October 12 land was sighted, probably what is now Watling Bay in the Bahamas. After stopping to take on fresh water, Columbus sailed on, visiting Cuba and Hispaniola (Haiti and Dominica), where he founded a small colony. He then set sail to return to Spain on the *Nina* – the *Santa Maria* having been wrecked in a storm.

In mid-March 1493, Columbus sailed triumphant into Spanish waters and when he landed was hailed as a hero. Six months later he was off again – this time commodore of a much larger fleet of 20 ships. Three years later, he was back in Spain, having sighted Dominica. But he was a broken, dejected man. The voyage had been marred by a succession of wretched quarrels with his crew and by a serious illness that had laid him low for months in Hispaniola.

Columbus wasn't the sort of man to stay down for long. 1498 saw him back at sea again on a voyage that resulted in the European discovery of the South American mainland. Two years later, after a furious quarrel with the newly appointed Spanish governor of the islands Columbus had discovered, he and his brother Bartholomew were sent home to Spain in chains. However Ferdinand and Isabella, grateful for the wealth that was beginning to flow in from their new territories on the other side of the Atlantic, restored him to favour and sponsored his last great voyage, which lasted from 1502 until 1504. During this time his ships sailed along the south coast of the Gulf of Mexico.

Again, politics and plotting marred the voyage and when Columbus returned to Spain, he found that powerful enemies were working against him at court. He withdrew from public life and died in a Spanish monastery in 1506. His remains were eventually taken to Hispaniola where they reposed for more than 250 years before being re-interred in the cathedral in the Cuban capital, Havana. At the end of the nineteenth century they were returned to Spain and in 1902, with great ceremony, were deposited in an ornate tomb in Seville cathedral.

Christopher Columbus, the man who made the European discovery of many Caribbean islands, of South and part of Central America, made one huge mistake. To the end of his days, he refused to believe that he had discovered a new continent. He insisted that what we now know to be South America was the east coast of India and that the islands on which he landed or sailed passed, lay off the Indian coast. Which is why many of the Caribbean Islands, that lie off the *east* coast of the *American* continent, are collectively called the West Indies.

C. 1520s

THE ATLANTIC OCEAN

Hot chocolate

Among the many things to be introduced into Europe from South America was chocolate. It quickly became popular in Spain but was much slower to catch on in other European countries, particularly in England where people who did see cocoa beans were so put off by their resemblance to sheep droppings that they refused to believe that anything good could come of them!

So widespread was the distaste for it in England, that when English privateers, ships granted permission from the crown to board enemy ships and confiscate their cargoes, found cocoa beans in the holds, they tipped them overboard rather than give them valuable space in their own holds.

It wasn't until John Gage, an English sailor who had been imprisoned by the Spanish, advised his fellow countrymen to flavour chocolate with rosewater, cinnamon and other such things that the English started to acquire a taste for the stuff. Now almost five hundred years after goodness knows how many tons of chocolate were sent to the bottom of the Atlantic Ocean, they can't get enough of it!

1574

THE NETHERLANDS

William the Forever Silent

In the eleventh century, the Netherlands was brought under the rule of the dukes of Burgundy, by purchase, inheritance and conquest. In 1519, Duke Charles succeeded his grandfather to become Holy Roman Emperor and the country came under Spanish rule – or misrule as it turned out to be. By the middle of the sixteenth century, opposition to Spain was such that in 1579, led by William the Silent, the northern provinces of the Netherlands united to resist Spanish rule. They were so successful that Philip III of Spain had little option but to agree to a truce. To the Dutch, William was a hero. To the Spanish he was a heretic, and despite the truce, Philip put a price of 25,000 ecus (a currency of the day) on William's head, with the result that several attempts were made on the Dutch prince's life.

In March 1582, Juan Juareguy, a Catholic assassin, fired a pistol at William from such close range that he set the royal hair and beard alight. William's wound would have been fatal had it not been for the loyalty and devotion of William's servants who, for seventeen days, took it in turns to hold it closed with their fingers until it started to heal and William was out of danger.

Later in the same year, two attempts, funded by the Duke of Parma, William's arch enemy, were foiled. But the threats came not just from Spain. One of William's own countryman, a young zealot named Hanzoon, twice tried to blow him up at his palace.

In 1583, a young Calvinist Frenchman, Francis Guyan, attached himself to William's court. Guyan's father, the young man told the prince, had died fighting in France. William was so impressed by the Frenchman's sincerity that he sent him on a diplomatic mission to France. But a little time later, he noticed that Guyan was still in Holland. When he asked why, Guyan told the prince that he had neither shoes nor clothing of good enough quality to wear on such a mission. The generous William gave Guyan twelve crowns from his own pocket to buy what was necessary.

On 10 July, 1584, William was at his palace, Prinsenhof, enjoying the company of family and close friends when Guyan stepped forward and shot him in the chest. The Dutch prince died within minutes having made not one but two fatal mistakes.

The first was not checking Francis Guyan's credentials. He was French, certainly, but far from being a Calvinist, he was a devout Roman Catholic. His name was not Francis Guyan, but Balthazar Gerard. And his mission to assassinate William had been encouraged by the Duke of Parma.

William's second mistake was lending Gerard money to buy clothes and shoes. The young Frenchman had arrived at court determined to kill William but lacked either sword or pistol to do the deed! The money he was given by William, he used to buy two pistols – from one of William's own guards!

Gerard was duly executed for his crime. He was flayed alive and then red-hot pincers were used to tear the flesh from his bones. Not content with that, and while he was still alive, the Dutch then disembowelled him and finished the job by cutting his body into quarters.

Shortly afterwards, the guard who had innocently sold Gerard the pistols with which William was assassinated also paid for his mistake by committing suicide.

1603

LONDON

Death of a painted lady

In March 1603, Queen Elizabeth I was dying, but almost to the end she refused to do two things – take to her bed or remove her make up. For years she had gone to great lengths to achieve the white pallor that had been fashionable among aristocratic women for several years. It was only after she died and the make up was removed that the ravages not just of time were revealed . . .

Sixteenth-century women applied powders, lotions and potions to their faces and other exposed parts of their bodies not just to acquire 'the look' but to cover freckles, spots and worse, the ravages of smallpox. Make up had become popular with the increasingly widespread use of the looking glass in the Middle Ages. Although cosmetics were condemned by the Church as being the tools of the Devil, women peered into the glasses, saw the spots and pock marks in close up and reached for the bottles – and the most popular of them was Venetian ceruse.

Aristocrat women all over Europe, including Catherine de Medici, Queen of France, paid for the honour of learning about and testing cosmetics containing this particular elixir. They applied layers of potions containing the stuff to their faces, shoulders and arms, necks and cleavage – anywhere where men's eyes may stray. And not discrete, thin layers – they painted Venetian ceruse on as thickly as some artists lay oils on their canvases. And fifteenth and sixteenth-century women were not as fastidious in matters hygiene as their twenty-first century cousins. Rather than remove make up at the end of the day and re-apply it the next morning, they painted one coat on top of another until, in the words of a contemporary monk, they looked 'ugly, enormous and abominable'.

As the years passed, other colours – reds, yellows, even greens – were added the aristocratic woman's personal palette, and the cosmetics that were applied to create them continued to be based on Venetian ceruse. In England, Queen Elizabeth set the tone, and if she painted her face then so did the ladies of her court. The older she got the more she applied

Regal: *Queen Elizabeth I and Sir Walter Raleigh*

until, as modern historian Geoffrey Regan, writes, 'she resembled a ship's figurehead, worn from storm and battle, with the paint peeling off'.

Elizabeth did not only use Venetian ceruse. To redden her cheeks she rubbed them with mercuric sulphide. It was only when she died and her mask was finally removed, that the ravages not so much of time, but of the very cosmetics she had used to disguise them, were revealed. For Venetian ceruse was made from white lead and was extremely poisonous when absorbed through the pores of skin, rotting the teeth of the women who used it and ageing the skin horribly.

They had been warned. One sixteenth century scribe had written that Venetian ceruse, 'wears them out and makes them grow old before their time . . . destroys their teeth, while they seem to be wearing a mask all the year through'.

But despite the awful example of Elizabeth, women continued to paint their faces with damaging cosmetics, in the mistaken belief that the look would make them more attractive to their menfolk. One potion that was sold successfully for well over 200 years was Solomon's Water. The quacks who sold it claimed that it would clear the skin of all impurities – spots, freckles, moles, warts and pock marks. It did – but as it contained sublimate of mercury, when applied over-enthusiastically it stripped the skin off the face, ate into the flesh and, like Venetian ceruse, made the gums recede and teeth to fall out.

To be fair, some women did heed the warnings and rather than paint their faces, drank potions that were 'guaranteed' to achieve the modish pallor. At best all that the concoction of ash, coal dust and candle wax did was to turn the drinker green and make her vomit, which probably did add a fashionable whiteness to the complexion. At worst it killed her.

Throughout the seventeenth, into the eighteenth century and beyond, women applied lethal, lead-laden concoctions to their face, sometimes with fatal results. In 1767, Kitty Fisher, a well-known actress and courtesan, died of lead poisoning caused by her injudicious use of ceruse. And that was seven years after the death of a woman who Kitty would undoubtedly have heard off – Maria, Countess of Coventry. A famous beauty of her day, she thought beauty was everything and clung to it by applying inordinate amounts of ceruse to her face. Her health slowly declined, but nothing would make her stop. Day after day she would recline on her chaise-long, looking glass in her hand, scanning her white, mask-like face for any imperfection. And when she saw one, real of imaginary, her fingers would dip in the ever-ready pot of ceruse . . .

Eventually she became so withered and haggard that she took to her room and ordered the curtains to be forever drawn so that no one could see her in daylight. When she died 10,000 people turned up for her funeral. But had they been able to see the bald, toothless, wrinkled old crone of a countess who lay in her coffin, none of them would have recognized her as the beautiful Maria Gunning who had dazzled society only a few years before.

1624

THE EAST COAST OF NORTH AMERICA

The bargain of the centuries

In 1624, Dutch settlers in the New World decided they wanted to build a town on the island at the mouth of the River Hudson. Peter Minuit, a representative of the Dutch West India Company, approached a group of locals and traded the land for some beads and trinkets worth about 60 Dutch guilders, or about £16.00.

Everyone was happy with the deal: the Native Americans did not regard land as something to buy and sell, it was just there to use like air and water; the Dutch got what they wanted and set about building on the land they now owned.

The island was Manna Hattin, today better known as Manhattan and worth an almost incalculable amount of money. A great bargain for the Dutch who called the city they built there New Amsterdam. A big mistake for the Canarsie Indians. But if they had held out for cash and invested their money in a bank and left it there, it would be worth around $50 billion today.

1628

STOCKHOLM

A gun or two too many

Sweden has had few more powerful kings than Gustavus Adolphus. He was a capable and popular king, at least until the expensive wars in which Sweden became embroiled during his reign led to crushing taxation and economic turmoil. It was typical of the man that in 1625 when Sweden was at war with Poland, he decided to frighten the pants off the poor Poles by building what was to be the biggest battleship in the world. It was also typical of the man that the name chosen for this titan of the Baltic was to be *Vasa* – his own surname!

Work started. Well over 1,000 oak trees were axed to make the hull. Countless pine trees were chopped down to provide the masts and planks for the decks. Over 1,000 square meters of cloth was woven to make the sails. And when everything else was ready, the guns were brought aboard – sixty of them: many more than any other warship.

Three years after work had begun, *Vasa* was ready. She was towed from the shipyard into Stockholm's beautiful harbour, which was lined with crowds whose cheers almost drowned out the music being played by several brass bands. To acknowledge the tumultuous welcome, the captain ordered several salvos to be fired and then set a course for open waters.

As soon as *Vasa* cleared the confines of the harbour the sails were unfurled and, gathering speed, the ship made to sail into the Baltic. Suddenly a strong gust of wind heeled her over. With their cheers dying in their throats, the horrified burgers of Stockholm watched as *Vasa* slid beneath the waves and sank to bottom of the sea where she lay until 1961 when she was raised to the surface, later to be displayed in a specially built museum in Stockholm.

Gustavus Adolphus's mistake was his decision to fit the ship with 60 guns, which made her top heavy. A few guns less and she would probably have sailed into battle and wrought havoc on Polish shipping. He also paid the price for ignoring the example of Henry VIII's flagship *Mary Rose*, which suffered a similar fate in 1546.

Overgunned: *Gustavus Adophus gets carried away equipping his new flagship with cannon*

1666

LONDON

The baker dun it

Situated in the centre of an overcrowded part of the city, close to the main road that led to London Bridge, Pudding Lane was best known as an unsavoury dumping ground for unsold or unwanted meat from nearby Eastcheap Market. No one of much importance lived there in the middle of the seventeenth century. There was a baker's shop in it, owned by John Farynor, and an inn.

After many years of Roundhead rule, Londoners had taken Charles II to their heart when the monarchy had been restored in 1660. At that time, fires were common in the city, but they usually burned themselves out or were easily contained before they did too much damage. Even so, it was something that troubled the king and in 1665 he wrote to the city's lord mayor, asking him to impose more stringent fire regulations. The mayor did little: he was more concerned with the plague that swept through the city in 1665.

Late on 1 September the following year, John Farynor went to bed as usual in the room above his bakery. After snuffing out the candle he settled down for a good night's sleep. History doesn't record whether or not he was married. If he was perhaps his wife asked him if he had damped down the ovens, and perhaps he yawned and said he had. He hadn't. As least not properly.

At around two in the morning the flames in the oven started to spread to the rest of the shop and a few minutes later the place was ablaze. Sparks from the fire set bales of straw piled up alongside the neighbouring Star Inn ablaze and soon it was being licked by flames.

As the fire spread, crowds gathered to watch, no doubt enjoying the spectacle. The mayor was summoned and was quite unfazed by the blaze. 'Pish!' he is reported to have exclaimed, 'A woman might piss it out'.

An hour after it started, the fire had taken grip. Among those who were stirred from their sleep was Samuel Pepys. 'I rose and slipped on my nightgown,' he wrote in his famous diary, 'and went to her [his maid's] window and thought it to be at the backside of Mark Lane at the farthest and so to bed again and asleep'.

In the morning Pepys set off for his office in the Admiralty and told his colleagues about the fire when he got there around noon. Later, the king was informed.

The Lord Mayor's hopes that the fire would burn itself out were soon dampened. The blaze spread and spread, and by mid-afternoon it had reached the warehouses that lined the banks of the River Thames. Packed with coal, brandy, oil and timber, they exploded like bombs.

Fanned by a steady, dry wind blowing in from the east, the fire spread westwards. At one point late on Sunday evening the flames were almost brought under control, but so slowly were the taps running that the fire fighters cut the water pipes so that they could fill their buckets more quickly. Unfortunately this completely cut off the water supply in the area and the flames took hold again.

By the following day, people were leaving the city in their thousands. The roads out of town were crammed with Londoners, pulling handcarts piled high with as many of their possessions they could load on them. Among those in the crowd was Samuel Pepys 'With one's face in the wind,' he wrote, 'you were almost burned with a shower of fire drops from this most horrid, malicious, bloody flame . . . smoke was so great as darkened the sky at midday. If at any time the sun peeped forth it looked red like blood'.

On Wednesday, the fire was brought under control thanks largely to the king who ordered fire-fighters to create a firebreak by knocking down buildings that lay in the blaze's path. By then, 13,000 houses had been destroyed, 87 churches lay in smouldering ruins and 300 acres of the city had been transformed into little more than a blackened desert. Sparks from burning shops on London Bridge were carried across the River into Southwark starting hundreds of fires. Thankfully they were all small and easily contained. But back on the north of the Thames, The Guildhall and the Royal Exchange had burned to the ground.

Most famously of all St Paul's Cathedral had been destroyed. The heat there was so great that some of the old tombs burst open to reveal their gruesome contents. The lead roof melted and molten metal flowed down the surrounding streets.

Surprisingly, only eight people died in the Great Fire of London, but it was not until six months after it started – courtesy of one simple mistake by a baker – that the embers stopped smouldering.

The Fire did have some benefit for the city. Sir Christopher Wren and his assistant Nicholas Hawksmore designed some beautiful churches to replace the ones that had been lost. The jewel among them was the new St Paul's Cathedral, one of the loveliest buildings in London.

That was for later generations of Londoners to enjoy. For those who lived in London in 1666, there were more immediate benefits. Acres of unhygienic slum housing had been destroyed and had to be replaced. The king ensured that better fire safety regulations were put into effect, but perhaps best of all the fire finished off the Great Plague in which 100,000 Londoners had died.

1685

LONDON

Curing the king

One Sunday in early February 1685, when King Charles II was 55, he fell ill. His doctors ordered that the curtains in his bedchamber be drawn and got to work. As was usual, they drained blood from cuts they made in his shoulders. Not satisfied with the blood that dripped in the cups from these wounds, they tapped into veins all over his body. They even shaved his head to draw some from the veins there.

When he didn't rally, they coated his feet with a poultice made from pitch and pigeon dung. Then, to 'cure the humours from his brain' they blew hellebore (a partly poisonous plant) up his nostrils to make him sneeze. That done, someone suggested that perhaps by making the king sick would clear his belly. So they made him swallow a mixture of antimony and sulphate. The king duly threw up, but still didn't get better.

'Maybe if we emptied his bowels,' someone suggested. So they gave him purgative after purgative. The royal bowels were soon empty of everything in them.

For five days, they gave him tonics when he went into spasms and gargles when he started to complain of a sore throat. They gave him tonics for his heart, and when he rallied a little and said he was hungry.

The only thing that they did that had any effect was to give him Peruvian bark when his temperature started to soar.

Through all of this, the king remained quite lucid, putting up with everything with a remarkable good humour. Even on the Friday night, after he had tolerated his doctors' lotions and potions for five days, when they decided to take even more of his blood, he put up no resistance.

He died the following morning.

With hindsight, we now know that Charles was in the terminal stages of an incurable kidney disease. But as one of his biographers has it, 'He was denied only three things – light, rest and privacy. Nothing else was left untried'.

1685

LONDON

Dead like him!

Aristocratic rebel: *the Duke of Monmouth*

In 1685, James, Duke of Monmouth, the illegitimate son of Charles II, landed in the West Country, and raised a small army in an attempt to take the throne from the Roman Catholic James II. The revolution failed dismally and Monmouth was sentenced to death by beheading. The executioner was obviously not up to the job, for it took five blows of the sword before the ducal head was separated from the shoulders.

But the most macabre

mistake of the whole bungled incident occurred later when the Keeper of the King's pictures found that there was no official portrait of Monmouth, which, convention demanded, there should be. To make good the oversight, Monmouth's decapitated head was stitched back onto the body, which was seated in a suitable chair and then committed to canvas by Sir Geoffrey Kneller, the German-born court painter.

1687

PARIS

Conducting his own death

In the days before the German composer and conductor Louis Spoor introduced the baton in 1820, conductors kept tempo by beating a heavy staff on the floor. Almost 250 years before Spoor's innovation, the Italian-born composer Jean Baptiste Lully, director of music a Louis XIV's court, was conducting

Beating time: *German conductor Louis Spoor*

a *Te Deum* in Paris. Unfortunately he struck himself in the foot and an abscess developed. A few days later, gangrene set in and Lully died of blood poisoning a few weeks later.

1689

WINDSOR

The pillars of Wren's wisdom

When the men who commissioned Sir Christopher Wren to design the interior of the Guildhall in Windsor saw the finished result they thought that there were not enough pillars to support the ceiling, so they ordered Wren to add some more. Wren disagreed but rather than argue the point, he put up four dummy pillars that serve absolutely no structural purpose: in fact, they do not even reach the ceiling, they just look as if they do. The optical illusion fooled the good men of Windsor and generations of visitors who have admired Wren's Windsor Guildhall ever since.

Master builder: *Sir Christopher Wren, architect extraordinaire*

1720

HAMBURG

A musical blunder

There were several candidates for the post of organist at the Church of St James in the baroque city of Hamburg, in Germany. Among them was a visitor to the city who had dazzled audiences with his brilliant performances and compositions. The church elders decided to hold a competition, but the young man told them that he was engaged to play elsewhere at the time the competition was to be held. They had all heard him play and he thought that he was not stepping across the line when he told them that should they offer him the job, he would accept.

But the competition went ahead and when the result was announced, the congregation was astonished, for the winner was not the young virtuoso but the little known and much inferior Johann Joachim Heitmann. It later transpired that he had assured himself of the job by promising to make a donation of 4,000 marks to the church should he be appointed.

And the young organist who should have got the job? He went off to Leipzig where he made a name for himself. Johann Sebastian Bach!

1724

EDINBURGH

' . . . Until presumed dead!'

In the early 1790s a young Edinburgh woman, Margaret Dickson, decided she had had enough of marriage and motherhood and set off to better herself. Leaving her husband and two children behind, she set off for Newcastle where she knew she would find a sympathetic ear from her two aunts who lived there. A few days later, she had reached the small village of Maxwellheugh, not far south from Kelso where she decided to stay for while, accepting the offer of a job in service to a family called Bell.

The reasons for this have never been made clear. Perhaps she was worn out after walking and hitching rides on passing carts for so long. Maybe she started to believe that her aunts might not turn out to be so sympathetic as she thought. Or maybe it was something to do with her employer's son, William, by whom she had a baby nine months later! Margaret claimed she had been raped while she slept: William claimed she had been more than willing to take to his bed. Whatever the case, on December 1723, the body of a newborn infant was found by William's brother in the River Tweed.

Margaret, who had done

Gloaters: *crowds assemble for a public execution, Scotland*

her best to conceal her pregnancy, confessed that the baby had been hers but claimed it had been stillborn and that she had kept the body hidden in her bed for eight days after her futile labour was over.

Her story was not believed. If the baby was stillborn, why had she kept it for so long before disposing of it in such a heartless manner? She was taken to Edinburgh, tried for murder and, when found guilty, sentenced by the black-capped judge to hang by the neck until dead. On September 2, she was taken to the Grassmarket, a tenement-lined open space that sits in the shadow of Edinburgh Castle, where several thousand people watched her mount the gallows, have the rope put round her neck and then drop into space when the trapdoor was opened.

Her body was left hanging for about thirty minutes, the hangman tugging her legs several times to make sure she was dead. When he was convinced she was, he had her body cut down and put into a coffin, which was given to her friends. They put it on a cart to take it to Musselborough, a small village to the east of Edinburgh.

During the journey, the funeral procession was attacked by a gang of thugs who made their living out of selling corpses to Edinburgh surgeons for dissection. In the ensuing scuffle, the coffin, which had been sealed, was damaged. Margaret's friends put the attackers to flight and continued on their way.

When they reached a small hamlet called Peppermill, they adjourned to an inn for refreshment, leaving the coffin outside. A few minutes later, a group of local youths who were gathered round the coffin, heard noises coming from it. Horrified, they rushed into the inn to alert the coffin bearers and get them to open the coffin. The lid removed, Margaret's friends were horrified to see her limbs twitching. To test that she was indeed still alive, one of the men took his penknife from his pocket and cut into one of her veins. Slowly, blood began to trickle from it and a few moments later Margaret groaned 'Oh, dearie me . . .'

As gently as they could, Margaret's friends removed her from the coffin and laid her on the side of the road. Slowly, the blood returned to her marmoreal cheeks and blue lips. A little later she was helped onto the cart and taken to Musselborough where over the next few days she recovered from her ordeal, so much so that on the following Sunday, the officially dead woman was well enough to attend church.

Crowds flocked to see the celebrated Margaret, including her husband with whom she was soon re-united. Under Scottish law, the sentence of the court had been carried out – Margaret Dickson had been hanged by her neck until [declared] dead. For her part, she was so grateful that she vowed to spend one day a week fasting and praying for the rest of her life – a vow she is said to have kept.

If the Edinburgh hangman had not made the mistake of declaring Margaret dead and had kept her hanging there for longer, no one would have heard of her. As it is, she is still known in her native village as the woman who beat the hangman.

1720

LONDON

A bubble that was bound to burst

Since trading in stocks and shares first got underway – the world's oldest Stock Exchange is in Amsterdam where dealings in printed shares of the United East India Company of the Netherlands began in 1602 – many mistakes have been made. People have bought shares in the belief that they would increase in value many times, only to see their investment wiped out almost as soon as it was made. If the road to hell is paved with good intentions, the road to ruin is paved with bad investments. And nowhere was this more true than in Britain in 1720 . . .

George I had come to the throne in 1714 on the death of Queen Anne. George, a prudent German, frowned on the British national debt and was keen that it should be paid off. Even then, the British monarch's power lay in the influence it could wield rather than on any direct action it could take. But even so, George invited two financial institutions to suggest ways to eliminate the debt – the Bank of England, founded in 1694 by a Scotsman, George Paterson, and the South Sea Company.

The South Sea Company had come into existence as a result of British (mainly English) jealousy of the vast wealth that the Spanish derived from gold and silver mines in their South

American colonies. Almost since the first *conquistadors* had cut a swathe through Mexico and Peru, precious metals had flooded across the Atlantic into Spanish coffers. For years, the English had watched enviously as the Spanish treasury bulged with South American bullion, but all their attempts to gain a foothold in this lucrative trade had come to nothing.

But after British victories in the War of the Spanish Succession, Spain was forced to concede what became known as the Asiento Contract. Under this agreement one English ship a year was granted permission to trade with Mexico, Peru or Chile: a condition of the concession being that the King of Spain was paid a quarter of all profits. The trading company created to operate the trade was the South Sea Company.

Responding to George's invitation regarding ways of paying off the national debt, the company came up with the suggestion that they would raise £2 million by public subscription and use the money to fund the debt. In the public mind, the company and the fabled wealth of South American gold mines went hand in hand, and ignorant of the truth that the company had few contacts in the South Seas and made hardly any money by trading there, there was widespread enthusiasm for the scheme.

On 2 February 1720, the House of Commons, despite the warnings of Robert Walpole, accepted the plan. As stock in the Company started to rise at an astonishing rate – in one day alone it tripled in value – Walpole continued to warn of the dangers of investing in such a speculative venture. But few paid him any attention: people mortgaged their homes, pawned their jewels, borrowed from Peter (in the form of anyone who had money to lend) to invest in Paul (in the form of the South Sea Company).

The Company's Directors, keen to keep the price at an ever-increasing premium, began to whisper that a new treaty was being negotiated with the Spanish who were said to be on the point of handing over the Potosi silver mine in Peru to the British. The price went up again.

Then, it was learned that Spanish settlers in Mexico were so keen to buy English cotton and wool that they would pay previously unheard of amounts of gold for them. The price increased even further.

Soon trade in the Company stock was so heavy that the Stock Exchange became so crowded the streets around it were impassable to carriages. They became even more crowded when the Company suggested that Spain was so keen to recover Gibraltar, which had been ceded to Britain under the 1713 Treaty of Utrecht, that they were willing not only to exchange part of their South American colonies for it, but also revoke the Asiento contract and allow all the ships in the Company's fleet to have access to the South Seas.

It wasn't long before other companies began to jump on the bandwagon. Few of them lasted long – about a week was standard – but that was long enough for fortunes to be made (the Prince of Wales made £40,000 in one of them) and lost. These companies were appropriately enough known as 'bubbles' – bursting almost as soon as they had been floated. It didn't seem to matter what the stated aim of the company was – the public would invest in it. They even flocked to put their savings in a company that was formed 'for carrying on an undertaking of great advantage' despite the fact that no one was ever told what the undertaking actually was!

By June, the king had awakened to the dangers that such foolish speculation posed. He advocated laws be passed by which directors of 'bubble' companies were to be fined if their schemes turned out to be suspect.

By this time, the stock in the South Sea Company had continued to rise – doubling during May alone. At first a few, and then more and more investors realized that this was unsustainable. It was time to sell and take the profit. On 3 June, sellers outnumbered buyers at the Exchange so that the stock started to fall. The Directors stepped in and started to buy as much of the stock as they could afford. Confidence was restored – but not for long.

By August, with the stock at ten times what it had been six months before, people heard that Sir John Blunt, the Company's governor, had sold his holding. The bubble quivered. And when it was learned that his fellow directors had followed suit, it burst.

With thousands of investors facing ruin, Blunt and other officers of the Company were attacked in the street. There was talk that the government might collapse. King George, on holiday in his native Hanover, hurried back to London. Parliament was summoned to deal with the crisis. Five of the Company's directors were arrested, but before he could join them the Company Treasurer fled to France with the books. The Chancellor of

Rack and ruin: *the South Sea Bubble as seen by Hogarth*

the Exchequer, one of the champions of the Company, was arrested, expelled from the House of Commons and sent to the Tower of London.

The only person to come out of the affair with any credit was Robert Walpole. Thanks to him, investors were repaid a third of what they had lost and faith in parliament was partially restored. But that was no comfort for those for whom one third was not enough to save them from financial ruin, all because they had made the mistake of listening to their king and their parliament and investing in a bubble that was bound to burst sooner rather than later.

1774

COLBERG, GERMANY

Pas de pommes de terre

Ask any schoolchild, well, English schoolchild, who introduced the potato into England from the New World, and it's more than likely the answer you will get is Sir Walter Raleigh. In fact, it was Raleigh's fellow Elizabethan Sir Francis Drake who first brought the potato across the Atlantic and started the English culinary love affair with the humble root vegetable. Boiled, steamed, roasted, mashed, chipped – in any of its many guises the English eat their way through thousands of tons of them every month.

But our cousins on much of mainland Europe turned their noses up at the South American tuber - and thousands of them died as a result. For reasons best known to themselves, our French cousins believed that eating potatoes caused leprosy (an odd belief when one considers that leprosy had been common in Europe for centuries before the potato was introduced) and refused to eat them. Indeed, such was the suspicion in which potatoes were held that in 1619 they were banned in Burgundy, an example that was soon followed by other regions of France.

And not just in France. The

Swiss came to believe that potatoes caused scrofula – tuberculosis of the lymph glands – which people once believed could be cured by being touched by a king or queen. And in Germany, in 1774, the citizens of one Prussian town decided they would rather starve to death than eat the potatoes that Frederick II of Prussia sent them during a famine. Twenty-one years later when the Bavarian harvest failed, the good burgers of Munich refused to give potatoes a chance.

But back to France. Throughout the eighteenth century there were many times when food was so scarce that historians believe tens of thousands of people died rather than eat potatoes, so deeply had the belief that potatoes caused illness become ingrained. However, in 1814, a French food writer, Antoine Beauvilliers, committed what could have been culinary treason when he published a book praising English cooking. Some of his recipes read so well on the page that his countrymen decided to give them a chance. And so the French found that *dauphinoise'd*, *gratinee'd*, *sautéed ou vapeur'd, le pomme de terre* was for them after all – but only after thousands of their countrymen had starved to death rather than even think about eating a potato.

1780

AUSTRALIA

Ravenous immigrants

Seven years after Captain Cook made the European discovery of Australia, the American War of Independence broke out. Not all Americans were in favour of the war and many of those who weren't looked to the British government to help them settle elsewhere. Reports that the area around Botany Bay in the new colony was fertile led the British to contemplate settling refugee loyalists in America in Australia, but for various reasons the project was abandoned and instead it was decided to establish a penal colony there.

The prisoners were later followed by settlers, who sailed from Britain in search of a new life. There was room in the holds of some ships (both penal and civil) for livestock. And what better animals to take to the new country than rabbits? They breed quickly and are a good source of meat.

Inevitably, a few rabbits escaped from the confines of their hutches and ran into the wild. With few indigenous predators, acre after acre after acre of abundant food and with land that was ideal for burrowing in, the rabbits bred . . . and bred . . . bred. Before too long there were more rabbits than people and by the 1880s there were so many of them that they had become a serious menace to farmers, eating their crops before they were ready for harvesting. In some places, they ate so much that farmers had nothing left to sell: in others, they ate so much that what had been pasture or grazing land became desert. And there were areas where the rabbit warrens had become so extensive that the earth collapsed, forming deep ravines.

The Australians hunted rabbits, they trapped them, and they shot them. They roasted them, grilled them, stewed them, put them in pies – people came to loathe the very sound of the name, let alone enjoy the meat they provided.

Eventually, the problem became so bad that the Federal government deliberately introduced myxamatosis into the rabbit population. The disease attacks the rabbit's central nervous system and is fatal. Best of all, it spreads quickly.

Over a surpassingly short time, the rabbit population started to shrink and the problem seemed to be over. But, as with all diseases, there were some rabbits that were either naturally immune to it or who somehow survived it and built up an immunity. Gradually they began to re-establish the rabbit population and today in some parts of Australia things are as just as bad as they always were.

Whoever it was who decided that rabbits would be a good thing for colonists to bring to Australia made a huge mistake for which generations of Australian crop-growers and stockmen have paid dearly.

1789

PARIS

Sweet-talking queen

France in the late 1780s was in a dreadful mess. The economy was in a parlous state. Having been forced to fund expensive war after expensive war, the Treasury was on the verge of bankruptcy. Taxation was high which infuriated the middle classes. They were further aggrieved by the fact that political power lay in the hands of a corrupt few who paid, at best, lip service to demands from the educated bourgeoisie for a say in the running of the country. Food, which was already scarce, became even scarcer when the harvest of 1788 turned out to be the worst for years. Peasants, especially those in Paris and the other major cities, were starving.

All this had very little affect on the aristocracy who carried on living the lavish lifestyle they had enjoyed for centuries. At the centre of this self-indulgent elite was the Royal Family whose members were said to squander fortunes on their whims. The queen, Marie Antoinette, the Austrian-born wife of Louis XVI, was especially loathed. While the people starved in Paris a few kilometres from the royal palace at Versailles, Marie Antoinette was rumoured to feed sweets and cakes to the lambs she kept at her toy farm in the grounds of the palace.

As things worsened, she

became the focus of the people's anger and was even nicknamed 'Madame la Deficit' – the woman responsible for the Treasury's empty coffers.

As the winter progressed, things got worse, and when Marie Antoinette was told that the Parisians had no bread, her reported retort, 'Let them eat cake' turned simmering anger to fury.

Things came to a head on July 14, 1789 when a mob stormed the hated prison in the centre of Paris – the Bastille.

Generations have come to believe that this was a peasant-led riot. *Wrong!* The man who inspired the mob was Camille Desmoulins – a friend of the two more famous leaders of the French Revolution – Danton, (actually D'Anton, he dropped the apostrophe to disguise his middle-class background) and Robespierre. Desmoulins was an unlikely revolutionary. He was born into the landed gentry and was educated at the elite College Louis-le-Grand, the year below Danton and Robespierre. He was small, bisexual and said to be utterly irresistible to woman (he married the daughter of one of his would-be mistresses, neither woman objecting to the match). He also had an appalling speech impediment. Yet it was he, not some unknown peasant, who stirred the mob and moved them to take the prison.

Generations have also come to believe that when the Bastille was stormed, hundreds of prisoners streamed from its damp, dank cells, having been imprisoned at the whim of their aristocratic masters. *Wrong!* Contemporary records show that there was only a handful of men locked up there – most of them for bankruptcy.

The event sparked the French Revolution during which hundreds of aristocrats (and later Danton, Robespierre and Desmoulins) were sent to the guillotine. Among them, in 1791, was Marie Antoinette. The story of her last few days as a prisoner makes harrowing reading. Stripped of the last shred of her dignity, she was bundled on to a tumbrel and carried through the crowds to the guillotine, where, it has to be said, she met her fate with fortitude.

Marie Antoinette: *no cake please!*

On the way there, someone shouted, 'Let her eat cake!' The cry was taken up by the crowd. They were mistaken to do so. There is no record of her ever having said the words. The first reference to the phrase was in the 1760s, in Jean-Jacques Rousseau's *Confessions* – when Marie Antoinette was still a young girl at her mother Maria Theresa's court in Vienna. Rousseau tells the story of a 'great princess' who, when told that there was no bread for the peasants to eat, said, 'Qu'ils mangent de la brioche' – brioche being a sort of bread with a high butter content, and no doubt the only kind the princess had eaten. If the French queen ever did repeat the remark it was therefore meant kindly!

1796

AYRSHIRE

A cold way to go

Scotland's national poet, Robert Burns, was a hard-drinking, womanizer whose years of carousing weakened his health. His final illness, rheumatic fever, struck him after he had fallen asleep on the roadside after a drinking spree that had gone on for several days. Perhaps not realizing that his heart was in bad condition or that the poet was suffering from depression, the doctors came up with a novel cure.

He was told to stand up to his armpits in the sea every day. The water in the Solway Firth was bitterly cold and to get to the required depth took a long wade every day. Burns seemed to have responded to this curious treatment. 'It has eased my pains and strengthened me,' he said – shortly before he died of the exposure brought about by his time in the water.

1799–1813

MAINLAND EUROPE

Getting it in the back

Napoleonic Wars: *friendly fire was a problem for the French back then as well*

'Friendly fire', the sad fact of war whereby soldiers are shot at accidentally by their own side, is not a modern phenomenon. Goivoin Saint-Cyr, one of Napoleon's marshals, estimated that some 25 per cent of French infantry casualties during the Napoleonic Wars were caused by men in the second rank being shot in the back by those in the third rank. Surprisingly, the French refused to change their firing tactics until 1813.

1803

SYDNEY

Third time lucky . . .

Joseph Samuels was a murderer: of that there can be no doubt. After he had been sentenced 'to hang by the neck until dead' he was led from the dock back to his cell, there to await the executioner's call. On the morning that it came he was taken to the gallows where the noose was put round his neck. The trap door opened:

Samuels dropped through it – and the rope snapped.

His hands still tied, he was taken back to the platform by which time the trapdoor had been closed. A new rope was found, tied into a noose and put around Samuels' neck. The trap door opened again. He dropped through it again – and the rope snapped again.

Once more time, Samuels was led up to the platform and one more time the noose was placed round his neck. It was third time lucky – for Joseph Samuels. Once again as he dropped through the trap door the rope snapped.

Enough was enough. Even though he had been found guilty of murder, the authorities thought he had gone through such a terrible ordeal that they reprieved him.

1831

WOOLWICH

Remembering an accidental death

The precise circumstances are not a matter of public record, but on 14 April, 1831, artillery officer Major James Brush was accidentally shot by his orderly and died of the wounds. The epitaph carved on his gravestone records the sad event thus. 'Sacred to the memory of Major James Bush who was killed by the accidental discharge of a pistol by his orderly 14th of April 1831. Well done good and faithful servant'.

1842

NEW YORK

This way to the Egress

Showman: *Phineas T. Barnum*

American showman *nonpareil* Phineas T Barnum's freak show was so popular that having paid their dollar to see it the punters were reluctant to leave. Barnum had his barker to take up a megaphone and shout, 'This way to the egress'. In the mistaken belief that an egress was another exhibit, most of the customers went where they were bid, only to find themselves back on the street, next to the entrance. Barnum was pleasantly surprised to find not only that the crowd thinned as he had hoped, but that many of them were happy to pay another dollar to get back in again.

1850

WEIMAR, GERMANY

Here Comes the Bride

Since Wagner's opera *Lohengrin* was first staged in 1850, countless brides have walked down the aisle to what they believe to be the wedding march from the opera. Actually, the famous melody is played neither when the bride approaches the altar nor leaves it on her husband's arm. It comes several hours after the wedding when the couple retire to the bridal chamber to make their own little night music.

1851

LONDON

Getting off to a bad start

London's Great Exhibition, designed to show to the world that Britain was at the cutting edge of nineteenth-century technology, introduced British women to an innovation in the world of fashion – bloomers. The garment, with its short flared skirt and lower leg clad in frilly leggings, had been named after Amelia Bloomer, the publisher of a woman's magazine devoted to advocating women's rights.

On 6 October, manufacturers of the novel garb decided to promote it by holding a lavish Bloomer Ball at the Hanover Square Assembly Rooms in fashionable Mayfair. Only ladies wearing the new bloomers were to be admitted, but most of the ones who turned up were ladies of the night, well aware that the new look advertised their wares more daringly than anything they had previously worn when looking for customers.

Word soon spread among the Burlington Berties and Hooray Henrys of the day and they flocked to Hanover Square to take advantage of what was so obviously on sale there! Such a melee developed and so indecorous was the behaviour of many of those crammed into the rooms that the police had to

Bloomers: *the height of Victorian erotica, apparently*

be called to restore some sort of order.

Bloomers never quite got over the association with loose women that they acquired that night and it was only much later that trousers for women caught on.

1854

THE CRIMEA

A magnificent failure

In 1854, Britain and France went to war along with Turkey to prevent the Russians seizing Turkish territory, which would have given the Russian navy access to the Mediterranean – something that other European powers were anxious to avoid.

Armies of both sides faced each other in the Crimean Peninsula, which juts into the Black Sea.

The commander of the Light Brigade, one of the British battalions, was Lord Cardigan, the man after whom the loose-fitting woollen jacket-cum-sweater is named (apropos of nothing at all, another of the senior British officers in the Crimea, was Lord Raglan, after whom the sleeve was named!).

On October 25, 1854, while British and French troops were engaged in battle at Balaclava (sad to say there was no Lord of that name) Russian soldiers seized some British cannon. When they were spotted hauling it away to behind their lines, the British commander-in-chief Lord Lucan sent one of his aides, Captain Nolan, to order Cardigan and his brigade to recapture the guns.

Nolan reported later than

when Cardigan received the order he snapped, 'Guns, sir! What guns!'

Unfortunately, Lucan hadn't been specific about which guns he had been referring to. An impatient, arrogant man, he assumed that if he ordered that guns be recaptured, it would be

Valley of Death: *the Light Brigade charge the Russian guns*

obvious to which ones he was referring. Nolan looked toward the Russian lines, at the far end of the valley in which the fighting was taken place. Ignoring the fact that there were Russian riflemen and artillery on either side of the valley, he pointed to the distant lines and said, 'There, sir. There are your guns.'

Cardigan could hardly believe what he had heard. But, 'orders is orders' and despite his obvious misgivings, he mustered his troops – five regiments of experienced horsemen - and gave the order to charge. As they thundered towards the Russian line, Cardigan at their head, they were easy targets for the Russian guns.

Cardigan succeeded in reaching Russian lines. Only then did he stop, turn round and see the carnage in his wake. And only then did he realize that Nolan had mistakenly pointed to the wrong guns. And only then did he rally the men who had survived Russian cannon and gunfire and give the order to withdraw.

Watching from a ridge on the valley, was the commander of the French troops who turned to an aide and remarked, 'C'est manifique, mais c'est n'est pas la guerre (It's magnificent, but it's not war)'.

The Charge of the Light Brigade was immortalized by Lady Butler in a glorious painting that captures the excitement of cavalry charging at full speed, and by Alfred, Lord Tennyson, who had succeeded William Wordsworth as poet laureate a few years before. In his poem, 'The Charge of the Light Brigade' he wrote:

'Half a league, half a league,
Half a league onward,
All in the Valley of Death
Rode the six hundred.

Theirs not to make reply,
Theirs not to reason why,
Theirs but to do and die.

Into the jaws of Death,
Into the mouth of Hell
Rode the six hundred.'

Had it not been for the poem, the Charge of the Light Brigade would probably have become nothing more than a footnote to history. But thanks to the impression Tennyson created in his poem, generations of English-speaking schoolchildren have come to believe that the entire Light Brigade was wiped out on that October day. In fact, 637 men galloped into 'The Valley of Death' and more than 450 survived to tell the tale.

1858

THE ATLANTIC OCEAN

A difference of direction

In 1857, the first attempt was made to lay a cable under the Atlantic between North America and Ireland to allow radio communication to be established between America and Europe. It was decided that the cable should run between Newfoundland on the eastern seaboard of North America and Valentia in southwest Ireland – a distance of just over 2,900 kilometres. Spirally bound heavy-gauge wire, which engineers had assured the investors would be strong enough to withstand the strains, was chosen for the job. Sadly, the engineers were wrong and the wire snapped. A second attempt was planned for the following year.

The plan was for the British ship *Agamemnon* to set off from Ireland and the

Translatlantic: *the first cable to cross an ocean is laid between Britain and the USA*

American ship *Niagara* to sail from Newfoundland, each laying half the length of cable and that they would rendezvous in the mid-Atlantic where the two ends would be joined together.

The two ships steamed out of port, laying the cable as they went and duly met half-way across the ocean. The contract to manufacture the cable had been given to two separate companies, one American and one British. One would have thought on so important a project every detail would have been decided upon well in advance. Sadly, this was not the case. The Americans had made their cable with the 'lay' of the wire armouring running in the opposite direction to the one made by the British: one being 'right-handed' the other 'left-handed.'

The effect of this difference was that when one end of the cable was tightened, the other cable was loosened. Engineers aboard the ships contrived to join the two cables, but it was a botched job and within the space of a few weeks after a few faint messages had been sent and received, the ends loosened and the cable fell silent.

The venture lost investors £500,000, a sum worth many times that amount today. With such a fortune at stake one would have thought that the British and Americans, said to be divided by a common language, could have got it right! But it was another eight years before a cable was run from both sides of the ocean and the ends joined successfully together, uniting the two continents telegraphically.

1867

ALASKA

A lesson in cold selling

Seward's Folly?: *within a few years of the US purchase of Alaska, minerals, oil and gold had been discovered*

In 1741, Danish explorer Vitus Bering landed in Alaska and claimed the territory for his Russian paymasters. The fact that the land was already occupied by North American Indians and Inuits, as it had been for centuries, didn't bother either him or the Tsar.

Russian ownership made no difference to the natives. They carried on fishing and hunting and making the best of their barren, ice-bound land as they had for countless generations. Alaska was thousands of kilometres from Moscow or St Petersburg and few Russians, except for a handful of fur trappers and bear hunters, travelled there. And the Russian winters were bad enough: why would anyone want to go to Alaska, even in the brief summer when the weather improves a little? It was not until 1784, 43 years after Bering had landed, that they even bothered to establish a permanent settlement there.

In 1867, William Seward, acting on behalf of the United States government, approached the Russians and offered to buy their frozen, North American territory. The American's motive was purely political. It was less than one hundred years since they had finally freed themselves from European rule and they wanted the continent to themselves. Even though Alaska was a huge distance from Washington and separated from the rest of the United States by 1,600 kilometres of Canadian territory, the United States preferred that it belonged to them rather than an imperial European power.

The Russians agreed a price of $7,200,000, which worked out at around $5.00 a hectare. The United States government may have been pleased with the deal, the American people were less than happy. What, they asked, did they want with an inhospitable, mountainous land of dense forest, snow and ice? So cynical were they about the deal that for more than 40 years Alaska was commonly called 'Seward's Folly.'

But if there was a mistake, it turned out to be the Russians who had made it, not the Americans. For in 1897, gold was discovered in the Klondyke. Hardy prospectors headed for the area, their heads turned with fortunes to be made. It wasn't long before other valuable minerals were unearthed – copper, chromium, zinc, mercury, nickel and platinum. And then, vast oil reserves were discovered at Prudhow Bay off the coast of the Arctic Ocean. The American investment has reaped enormous dividends. Seward's Folly turned out to be the Sale of the Century.

1869

VIENNA

It wasn't all right on the night

Smarting at his country's defeat by France in the short war of 1859, Emperor Franz Joseph of Austria decided to have much of the centre of Vienna remodelled and rebuilt to rival the splendid new public buildings and boulevards that were changing the heart of Paris. Chief among the new buildings in Vienna was to be a new opera house. But even before it opened the Viennese, thinking that the building that was supposed to rival the elegance of Paris was squat and ugly, had dubbed it 'the sunken trunk'.

Worse, in the eyes of the Viennese who had a Teutonic eye for detail, the two architects Eduard van der Null and Siccard von Siccardsburg had topped the house with two winged horses. Not only was Pegasus unique in Greek mythology and two figures of him failed to make that point, the equine sculptures were too plump, too small and too ugly (they were later sold to an American tourist).

But it was on the first night that the true awfulness of the design became apparent to the Viennese citizens. Tickets for the gala performance of Mozart's *Don Giovanni* had changes hands for unheard prices, squeezing the pockets of the city's opera-lovers so hard that their eyes watered. When all of smart Vienna were in their seats, the emperor and his entourage took their places in the ornate royal box. The curtain was already raised, but even before the lights had gone down it was obvious that all was not well. People in the third and fourth galleries – where many of the smartest families in the city were sitting – were starting to complain loudly that they could only see a small part of the stage.

On walked one of the most celebrated actresses of the day, Charlotte Wolter. Dressed as the Spirit of Vienna, she started to speak a specially prepared prologue – a hymn to the virtues of the city. Unfortunately, the censor had objected to part of what had been written and the cuts on which he had insisted had left the filleted version making hardly any sense. Laughter and catcalls joined the chorus of discontent coming from the parts of the house where the view was so restricted that Wolter was nothing more than a voice that could hardly be heard.

The prologue finished, those who could see settled back in their seats to enjoy a grand procession with tableaux representing the various parts of the empire that lived together in a harmonious whole ruled over by the emperor. As the head of the procession began to descent the grand staircase at the back of the stage, the conductor signalled for the orchestra to begin playing. Unfortunately, the musicians seemed not to have been told about the procession and the opening notes of Don Giovanni floated round the auditorium.

Thinking that the opera was about to start, the house lights were dimmed and everyone in the procession was left to fight their way off stage as those involved in the opening scenes of the opera took their places in the wings waiting for their cue. It was too much for the emperor who slipped out of the royal box, soon followed by much of the audience.

It was also too much for Eduard van der Null. He hanged himself in despair. He was followed to the grave two months later by his partner in crime von Siccardsburg, who, railing from the criticism, suffered from a heart attack and died.

1872

WASHINGTON DC

A costly comma

In 1872, the US Congress passed a Tariff Act, later signed by President Ulysses S Grant, listing among other non-taxable items, 'fruit-plants, tropical and semi-tropical for the purpose of propagation and cultivation . . .' Well, that's what the legislators thought the new law read. But a typist had accidentally put in a comma instead of a hyphen after 'fruit'. The result was that fruit and plants, tropical and semi-tropical . . .' became legally exempt from import taxes instead of fruit-plants as had been intended.

Eagle-eyed lawyers claiming to act for the importers of relevant fruit

President Ulysses S. Grant: *always read before you sign!*

and plants spotted the mistake and sued the US Treasury Department for a refund of the tariffs that had been paid between the Act becoming law and the error being discovered. They were awarded three million dollars (worth at least a billion by today's values) in settlement, making it one of the costliest punctuation errors in history.

It turned out the lawyers were acting in the public interest. They used the money to finance the construction of the Culver Railroad Line in Brooklyn, which later became part of the New York City rapid transport system.

1879

SCOTLAND

A fatal oversight

Rising on the slopes of Ben Ui in the Scottish Grampians, the River Tay flows south and east for almost 200 kilometres before emptying into the North Sea just below Dundee. The river's estuary had long inconvenienced travellers travelling north and south, making any railway line between towns and cities on either side of the Tay impossible.

In 1863, an official proposal was made to bridge the river, and seven years later, the construction of an iron railway bridge across the Tay was authorized by Act of Parliament. The man appointed to take charge of the project was Thomas Bouch, a highly successful civil engineer with wide experience in railway construction. He had helped design the Lancaster and Carlisle Railway and had been resident engineer on the Stockton and Darlington Railways. As manager of the Edinburgh and Northern Railway from 1849 he had helped design 'floating railways' across both the Firths of Tay and Forth as well as overseeing the construction of almost 500 kilometres of railway in Scotland and the North of England. With several bridges under his belt, he was the ideal man for the job.

Bridge of the silvery Tay: *disaster strikes Scotland's most prestigious railway bridge, over the River Tay*

In 1878, eight years after the project had been given the go-ahead by parliament, the Tay Bridge was opened amid great public ceremony. Dundee's master of doggerel, William McGonagall celebrated the event with the immortal lines:

Beautiful Railway Bridge of Silvery Tay!
And prosperity to Messrs Bouch and Grothe
The famous engineers of present day,

Who have succeeded in erecting
the Railway
Bridge of the Silvery Tay..

A year after the opening, Bouch was knighted and given the freedom of the City of Dundee. Unfortunately in his studies, Sir Thomas had taken as read the work of fellow civil engineer, John Smeaton. In 1759, Smeaton had written a book, *The Natural Powers of Wind and Water to Turn Mills*, which was an explanation of a series of tables he had presented to the Royal Society in 1759. The book stated that 'high winds' exerted a pressure of six pounds per square foot, and 'very high winds' eight to nine pounds per square foot. This rose to twelve pounds per square foot during 'storms and tempests.'

Ignoring the fact that the phrases 'very high winds' and 'storms and tempests' are scientifically vague to say the least, Smeaton greatly underestimated the effect of wind power on structures such as Bouch's bridge. In the event his designs made no provision for continuous lateral wind bracing below the track. Indeed, the evidence that came to light later suggests that Bouch made absolutely no provision at all for the effects of high winds on the bridge.

On 28 December 1879, just over eighteen months after the Tay Bridge had been opened, there was a hurricane blowing through Dundee. Just as the gale was at its height, the Edinburgh Mail Train steamed onto the bridge. As it was crossing the central spans, the wind blew thirteen of them into the water, taking the whole train with them and killing all seventy of the passengers in its carriages.

A year later, Sir Thomas followed them to the grave, a

man as broken as the bridge he had designed.

In 2003, Dundee City Council added insult to injury when they decided to commemorate McGonagall by putting up plaques bearing lines from his poetry all over the city. Sadly they spelt 'beautiful' incorrectly: not once, but six times!

1887

LONDON

An offence to the weaker sex

Whoever described women as the weaker sex got it wrong – but that is a mistake that we will not be going into in the pages of this book! Rather, let us ponder the two mistakes Dr Octavius Sturges made when he wrote to *The Lancet* – the distinguished journal of the British medical profession. The subject of his missive was St Vitus Dance, a condition properly called chorea that affects the central nervous system – making those who suffer from it prone to uncontrollable, irregular, brief jerky movements. Sturges wrote that it was caused by 'over-schooling, excitement, home lessons and caning.' But he offended many women when he observed that, 'More than twice the number of cases were of girls than of boys, because of the smaller brain of the former and their more delicate organization'.

Sturges wasn't alone in his low opinion of women. At around the same time as Sturges penned his infamous letter, his contemporary Samuel Smiles, a Scottish philosopher, wrote, 'As for women taking the place of men in the work of active life and becoming either sailors, soldiers, barristers or other occupations or professions, the thought is unworthy of serious consideration'.

1890

ABYSSINIA (ETHIOPIA)

A shocking waste of money

Emperor Meneleck II, Lion of Judah and absolute ruler of Abyssinia, was very taken with the stories he heard about how efficient the new-fangled electric chair was. So impressed that he ordered three to be despatched to him from New York. He overlooked the fact that there was no electricity in his kingdom. Two of the useless chairs were consigned to the dustbin, but not one to be seen to waste money, the emperor used the third as a throne!

1890

LONDON

The moving wound

In *A Study in Scarlet*, Sir Arthur Conan Doyle's 1882 Sherlock Holme's adventure, the author gave Dr Watson, Sherlock Holmes' colleague, a wound in the shoulder – the result of an incident that happened during Watson's military service in India. Eight years later, the wound has moved as if by magic to Watson's leg.

THE 1890s

HAMPSHIRE

Sorry, My Lord!

There have been many examples of lovers' trysts going sadly astray thanks to a mistake by one or other of the parties involved. But few can have ended so embarrassingly as they did for Lord Charles Beresford, a young aristocrat who hobnobbed with the country set during the last decade of Queen Victoria's reign.

Redfaced paramour: *Lord Charles Beresford strikes a pose*

When staying with his friend Sir Charles Chute at Chute's beautiful house, The Vyne, in Hampshire, his eye was caught by a particularly attractive young woman, who made it clear that she returned his interest in spades.

An assignation was duly made for late in the evening by which time everyone would be in bed. When the appointed hour came, the young man crept down the oak-lined corridor to his soon-to-be conquest's bedroom which, she had whispered to him, was next to the Tapestry Room.

Anxious to speed things up, Lord Christopher slipped off his dressing gown as he opened the bedroom door and as he tiptoed towards the oak four-poster bed, he divested himself of his pyjamas. He raised the counterpane, slipped into bed and embraced the body lying there.

Either the young lady had a mischievous sense of humour of Lord Charles had misheard the whispered instructions. Either way, it is difficult to say who was more surprised – Lord Charles, or my lord Bishop of Chester whose scrawny arms struggled desperately to repel Beresford's amorous advances.

1886

SOUTH AFRICA

Selling himself short

George Harrison was one of those men who had one dream – gold. He had prospected for it in Australia and now, in July 1886, he was in Witwatersrand in South Africa. The gold rush there was at its height and countless thousands of men had broken their backs searching for the precious mineral. Not Harrison (at least not this time). One morning, he simply looked down at the stone he had almost tripped over and realized that it was a large nugget of solid gold.

He took the nugget to the man who owned the land, Gert Oosthuizen, who sent him to President Kruger to tell the president of the find, and that Harrison was of the opinion that the seam that he had recently stumbled upon was workable.

Harrison took the letter to the capital where he signed an affidavit that read:

*My name is George Harrison and I come from the newly discovered goldfields in Klipivier, especially from a farm owned by a certain Gert Oosthuizen. I have long experience as an Australian gold digger and I think it is a payable [*workable*] goldfield.*

Within 48 hours, a petition had been presented to magistrates who granted the request that Oosthuizen's land and a large area surrounding it should be proclaimed a public goldfield. The same magistrates granted Harrison claim Number 19.

The seam that touched the surface of the vaal where Harrison had found his nugget became South Africa's Main Reef. During the next century, the gold mines that were opened up in the area produced up to one million kilograms of gold every year – well over half of the world's total gold production. The township that grew around the area was later renamed Johannesburg, now South Africa's largest city and main commercial centre.

And what of Harrison, the man who literally walked into one of the richest gold seams ever discovered? Four months after he was granted his claim he sold it and moved to Bramerton, then the largest town in the Transvaal. Rumour has it that he was eventually killed by a lion. There is no record of what he did with the money he got for his claim. £10.

1890S

BEDFORDSHIRE

The butler did it

Young Winston: *sans trademark cigar*

In the early years of the twentieth century a promising MP caught the eye of Sir Julius Wernher, who recognized in the young parliamentarian a politician of considerable potential. The young man for his part was well aware that an aspiring politician can't know enough multi-millionaires (this is long before the days when any substantial donation to a political party is viewed with suspicion by opposition parties and the press alike). Accordingly he accepted Sir Julius's invitation to join a house party at the sumptuous Wernher mansion, Luton Hoo in Bedfordshire.

The weekend was going with a swing, particularly dinner on Saturday when a great deal of alcohol was being consumed. Chief

among the imbibers was the Wernher butler who was drunk as the proverbial lord by the time the main course was being served. The hostess put up with this until her major domo poured a sauceboat full of Hollandaise down her dress.

After indicating to a footman to bring her paper and pen, Lady Wernher scribbled a note to the butler, which she slipped into his hand unseen by the other guests. 'You're drunk,' the note read. 'Leave the room at once.'

The butler put the note on a silver salver and slowly made his way down the room to present it to guest of honour – Sir Winston Churchill.

1893

LONDON

An elementary mistake

Whenever any of us say the immortal words, 'Elementary, my dear Watson.' we are repeating a mistake of our own making: for Sir Arthur Conan Doyle never put the words in Sherlock Holmes' mouth. The closest he got to it was in *The Crooked Man*, a short story published in *Strand Magazine* and included in *The Memoirs of Sherlock Holmes* a year later, in 1894.

By the time the story was written, Watson had found

himself a wife and no longer shared Holmes' flat at 221B Baker Street. When Holmes calls on his old friend to ask for his help in solving a mystery, he observes that, judging from the ash on his coat, the doctor still smokes the same pipe tobacco and that he is just as busy as he always was. When Watson asks how Holmes knows this, the pipe-smoking detective replies that when busy, Watson takes a cab, when he is not, he walks. Watson's boots are dusty but not dusty enough to have been walking far. Ergo, he must have taken a hansom cab, ergo he must be busy.

'Excellent!' says Watson.

'Elementary,' says Holmes.

In the same vein, when we hear the words, 'You dirty rat!' a mental picture of James Cagney probably comes to mind. Not once, in the many movies in which Cagney played the gangster, did the words cross his lips.

And just one more example of words mistakenly attributed to the famous, we all know that in *Casablanca*, after Dooley Wilson plays *As Time Goes By*, Humphrey Bogart says, 'Play it again, Sam.' We are all wrong! Bogart has banned the pianist

Elementary: *Dr Watson, I presume*

from playing the tune because it reminded him of the love affair he had with Ingrid Bergman. Wilson is tinkling the tune when Bogart is out of the bar he runs, but stops when he sees Bergman. 'Play it, Sam!' is the actual line, said by Ingrid Bergman.

After Sam has played the song, and after Bogart has heard it, the craggy star says, 'You played it for her. You can play it for me.'

1901

FLORIDA

A long wait

When J. B. Brown was standing on the gallows, a rope around his neck having been convicted of murdering an engineer, an eagle-eyed official noticed at the very last minute that the wrong name had been written on the warrant. Whoever had filled it in had put the jury foreman's name where Brown's should have been. The execution was cancelled and commuted to life imprisonment. Twelve years later, another man confessed to the crime and Brown was freed. If the correct name had been written on the death warrant, Brown would have swung for a crime he didn't commit.

1912

OFF THE COAST OF NEWFOUNDLAND

Titanic mistakes

The sinking of the *Titanic* on her maiden voyage, is one of the most poignant of maritime disasters. A series of Hollywood and British movies, some of them worthy, some of them brilliant box-office blockbusters and at least one of them that should have sunk along with the eponymous ship, has kept it in the public consciousness for nigh on one hundred years.

But the sinking was not just a tragedy. It was also a catalogue of mistakes, some of them as titanic as the ship itself . . .

On April 10 1912, the *RMS Titanic*, at the time the largest and most luxurious ship ever built, set sail from Southampton on her maiden voyage to the United States, having embarked from Belfast a few days earlier. On board were 2,227 passengers and crew. The combined wealth of the first and second class passengers was over $600 million – a staggering figure today let alone in 1912!

A coal strike had kept many transatlantic liners in dock and many wealthy travellers who tried to book first-class passages on the Titanic had been forced to accept second-class berths. No matter. If the first-class cabins, salons and dining room would have

Sinkable: *the Titanic goes to her watery grave*

graced a potentate's palace, second-class accommodation was only a little less luxurious. Passengers dined off the finest porcelain and sipped their perfectly chilled champagne from glasses made of the best crystal.

Even the steerage passengers quartered in the bowels of the ship, many of them setting off for a new life in the United States, found themselves in accommodation they could only previously have dreamed of.

All of them – multi-millionaires and enthusiastic emigrants alike – shared one belief. The *Titanic* was unsinkable. Its owners, the White Star Line, claimed to have had it designed so that even if it was holed, it would still be seaworthy. *Mistake Number One.*

The designers had originally specified 50 lifeboats. This was later cut to 42 lifeboats, and then to 20. But that was four more than required under British maritime law for a ship of the *Titanic's* size. But given the liner's unsinkability, the lifeboats were there to reassure the passengers. If the ship had to be abandoned, there was no need for panic – assistance would get there in plenty time. *Mistake Number Two.*

The voyage proceeded even better than planned, with the ship making such excellent progress that its owners decided to press full steam ahead for port and a new transatlantic speed record. *Mistake Number Three.*

The evening of April 14 was just like the others had been. The sea was flat calm, the air was bracing and there was no wind. A carpet of stars shone undimmed from a moonless sky. Radio messages had been received from other ships of icebergs in the area, but full steam ahead had been ordered and full steam ahead it was to remain. *Mistake Number Four*

At 11.40pm, the lookout, Frederick Fleet, called out 'Iceberg right ahead.' and tugged hard three times on the crow's nest bell, confident that he had given enough warning for the pilot to take avoiding action. *Mistake Number Five.*

As the *Titanic* glided past the towering iceberg at around 20.5 knots the iceberg grazed her side, fatally gashing her.

Water cascaded into the bowels of the ship, breaking down the supposedly watertight safety doors. Realizing that the ship was far from unsinkable, the Captain ordered the crew to assemble passengers on deck and take to the lifeboats. There were 2,277 people on board and space for 1,178.

Rockets were fired. May Day signals sent out. But the radio officer on the nearest ship, which was just ten miles away and could have reached the scene quite quickly, had gone off duty: *Mistake Number Six*. And the officer on the watch thought that the distress flares were fireworks and didn't warn the captain. *Mistake Number Seven*!

Three hours later, the Titanic lay in pieces 12,460 feet down at the bottom off the ocean floor, 375 miles due east of St John's Newfoundland.

705 (mainly first-class female passengers) of the 2,228 on board survived – the others either went down with the ship, drowned in trying to escape or froze to death in the icy water – their tragic mistake being to embark on a ship said to be unsinkable.

1912
SUSSEX, UK
Piltdown Man

In 1911, Charles Dawson, steward of the Barkham Manor Estate near Lewes in Sussex and an experienced amateur palaeontologist, was excavating a shallow grave on Piltdown Common when he unearthed the fossilized remains of a human skeleton.

Dawson may have been an amateur but he was well respected in archaeological and anthropological circles. He had found the tracks of a prehistoric megalosaurus and was credited with the discovery of three previously unknown species of iguanodon, one of which had been named after him. Palaeontology had been Dawson's lifelong passion: when he was 21 he had been made a Fellow of the London Geological Society.

By the time he unearthed what was to become known as 'Piltdown Man' he had amassed a huge collection of fossils – thanks largely to local quarrymen who were paid handsomely by Dawson for any fossils they came across in the course of their work. Most of these fossils eventually found their way to London's Natural History

Faking it: *the skull of 'Piltdown Man' fooled experts for years*

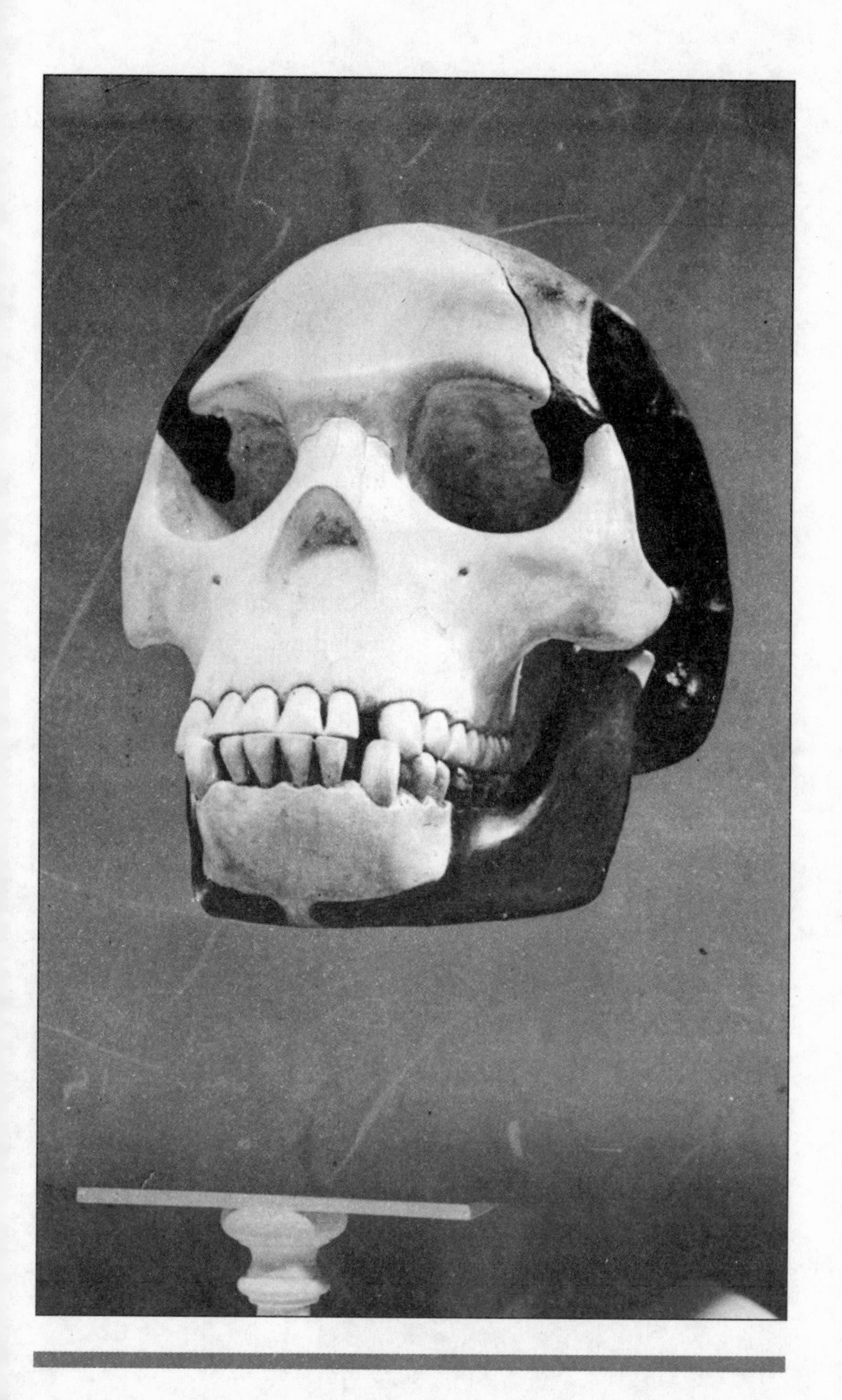

Museum where a 'Dawson Collection' was later established.

Dawson's version of events is that when he was walking on Piltdown Common one day in late 1911, one of the workman showed him what Dawson recognized as a piece of human skull. The workman said that while he and his fellow navvies had been digging, one of their spades hit a skull, which had shattered on impact. Dawson immediately began to look for more fragments and eventually found two more shards of skeleton, which he later took to the Natural History Museum.

There, Dr Arthur Smith Woodward, Fellow of the Royal Society and leading expert of fossil fish, urged him to look for more pieces as soon as he could. But winter rains had muddied the area badly and it was not until May the following year that Dawson was able to continue the search.

Accompanied by a Pierre Teilhard de Chardin, a Jesuit priest and enthusiastic palaeontologist (who later became one of the most respected philosophers in the Catholic church) Dawson found the rest of the skull bones and part of the lower jaw. De Chardin found some fossilized animal bones, including a canine tooth, and some typically crude flint tools.

Dawson, a keen reader on matters archaeo- and anthropological, was familiar with the work of German palaeontologist, Ernst Haekel, whose theory was that the stages in the embryonic development of many animals was similar to the evolutionary stages found in fossil animals. This would account for the fact that the skull Dawson found resembled that of a young chimpanzee, lacking the large protuberances of bone over the eyes typical not just of adult apes, but of fossil skulls of prehistoric man that had been previously discovered. When Woodward saw the skull discovered at Piltdown, he had no doubts. Charles Dawson had discovered a previously unknown species of prehistoric man.

Almost as soon as Woodward had made the discovery public at a meeting of the London Geological Society in December 1912, then news of it spread like wildfire through the scientific world. Dawson, it was claimed, had found the fossilized skull (considered to be that of a female) of one of a previously unknown species from which cave men and modern man had evolved.

Dawson died in 1916, honoured by his fellow palaeontologists as the man who had found the 'missing link' that confirmed once and for all that Darwin's Theory of Evolution' was valid. The species was named *Eoanthropus dawsoni* ['Dawson's man of dawn'] in his honour, although it was popularly known as 'Piltdown Man'.

Woodward, who was knighted in 1924, went on to expand on his original opinion. Judging from the shape of the jaw, it was beyond doubt that the creature had the power of speech, proving that 'in the evolution of the human species, the brain came first and speech was a growth of a later age.'

Woodward basked in the glory of Dawson's discovery, but in 1926 a detailed geological survey of Piltdown showed that its gravel pits were much more recent than had previously been supposed. Then, fossils found in Africa and Asia seemed to squeeze Piltdown Man out of the evolutionary equation.

And so the dust was blown off the remains that Dawson and Teilhard de Chardin had discovered in Sussex, and it was proved beyond all doubt that Piltdown Man was a fake – a skilful one, but a fake nonetheless. The cranium was human – but little more than 50,000 years old, the blink of an eye in palæontology terms. But the jaw was that of an orang-utan and the tooth that de Chardin had found probably came from a chimpanzee. And when the remains were subjected to chemical analysis, some of the fragments were found to have been smeared with compounds of chromium and others with iron sulphate. Neither of these substances occurred naturally in the Piltdown area. Another nail in Piltdown Man's coffin was that the teeth had been rubbed with some sort of abrasive to make them look as if they had become worn by natural human wear and tear.

So, it was established beyond doubt that Dawson's discovery was a fraud. What remains a mystery however is who was responsible and why. Knowing that the Sussex palaeontologist would pay handsomely for fossils, is it possible that the workmen could have planted them? Unlikely. So unlikely that we can dismiss it out of hand. Even if they had found the first fragments and planted the rest, none of them had the knowledge to know how to perpetrate such a skilled fraud.

Was it Dawson, desperately keen to be made a Fellow of the Royal Society, one of the greatest accolades to which a scientist can aspire? Did Dawson really believe that what he had found was genuine, but Woodward, keen to have a stunning feather in his cap, decided to try to deceive his fellow scientists? Indeed, was it a deliberate deception, or was it a simple hoax designed to make distinguished men on science look silly?

One thing we do know. Whoever created Piltdown Man, took the secret of his identity to the grave with him.

1915

SCOTLAND

Britain's worst train crash

Quintinshill was an almost unknown signal box near Gretna just across the Scottish border, sixteen kilometres from Carlisle. It would probably have remained unknown to everyone apart from those who lived nearby, had it not been for the chain of events that happened early one May morning during the First World War.

The Scots express train that had left London's Euston station at 11.45 the previous evening was running 30 minutes late as it approached Carlisle where it was scheduled to be handed over to engineers from Caledonian Railways to continue its journey north. Because the express was late, a northbound local train, which usually followed it, was despatched from Carlisle before it arrived. This was standard practice, because the local train provided a connection for Glasgow and Edinburgh at Beattock for passengers from Moffat, and the company was keen that it should keep to its timetable as closely as possible.

On this particular day, it was decided to send the local train forward as far as Quintinshill, which had lay-by loops on both the up and down side, where it was to be shunted to allow the two expresses to pass.

George Meakin, the duty signalman at Quintinshill had been on the night shift and was due to sign off at 6.00am, but he was still on duty at 6.30 thanks to a private agreement with the other signalman, James Tinsely, who was working the day shift. Whenever the local was going to stop at Quintinshill, as on this occasion, the signalman at Gretna gave Tinsely the tip off and he then travelled on it, getting off at the signal box. Meakin, meanwhile would write down all the train movements that occurred after 6.00 so that Tinsely could later copy them into the Train Register, making it appear that he had been on duty at the correct time.

When the local got to Quintinshill, there was a waiting goods train in the loop off the northbound track, and a train of Welsh coal trucks slowly running into the loop beside the southbound one. Meakin leaned from the signal-box and indicated that he was going to switch the local onto the southbound main line until the northbound express had gone through.

When the train had been

switched and was at a standstill on the southbound line, Tinsely and the fireman got down from the footplate and headed for the box where they were joined by the brakemen from the two trains in the loops. This was strictly against regulations, which stated that if the guard, brakeman or fireman of any train had to communicate information to the signal box, they should do so as concisely as they could, sign the Train Register and get back to their train as quickly as possible.

Tinsley handed Meakin the morning paper he had brought with him and as his friend settled down to read it, set danger signals on the north-bound track before beginning to copy Meakin's notes into the Register. Neither man wrote anything about the local that was on the southbound line.

Someone from Carlisle phoned through to tell Tinsley that the express that had been due at 6.05 had left 30 minutes late and was now on it way. After he took the call, Tinsley went on writing up the Register. A few moments later, the bell rang again – this time it was the signalman from Kirkpatrick, the next box up the line, asking for a clear track for a southbound troop train. Meakin told Tinsley that he had been expecting it: that was why he had shunted the Welsh train into the loop.

The troop train was packed with soldiers – fifteen officers and 470 other ranks from the 1st/7th Royal Scots, on their way from their training camp at Larbert in Stirlingshire to Gallipoli. They should have already been at sea, but their ship, *Aquitania*, had got stuck in the Mersey mud at Liverpool.

At 5.00am, when the train

steamed through Carstairs, the entire town had lined the track to wave the boys on their way to the front. The men had acknowledged the cheers then settled back to snooze, play cards or maybe just sit and ponder about what waited them at the front.

When the bell in the signal box announced that the troop train was entering Quintinshill's section, Tinsely sent his own signal to Gretna, which agreed in turn to accept it. Distracted by the chatter of the others and with the urgent task of fiddling the Register still to be finished, he reached for the signal-lever controlling the southbound main line and gave the all-clear – *even with the local in full view just below him.*

No sooner had he moved the lever, than the bell rang again. The express had passed through Gretna and was hurtling towards Quintinshill. Accepting the train, Tinsley gave the north line the clear signal: both lines were now signalled as clear.

Meanwhile, the troop train had been gathering speed as it sped down the gently graduated five-kilometre straight south of Beattock. The driver had a clear view of the line ahead, right down to where it curved under a bridge near the signal box. The driver and firemen probably noticed the huddle of trains by the signal-box but they would have assumed they were all in the loops – the signal was clear after all. The goods train in the south siding probably obscured their view of the main line, but once they were round the bend, the view would be clear again.

Doing a good 110km/h, the troop train raced down the slight gradient, steamed under the bridge . . . and slammed into the local train on the line ahead.

The impact was heard for miles around. The local train was thrown 40 metres backwards. The troop-train's coaches telescoped and were crushed forward. Its tender twisted around, pulling the splintering coaches with it and spewing wreckage onto the parallel northbound line. Seconds before the collision, the troop-train had been 200 metres long: the impact reduced it to well under half that length

In the box, the petrified signalmen stood frozen to the spot for a moment, watching the carnage below. Suddenly Meakin screamed, 'Where's the 6.05?' He dashed to the levers to set the signal to danger. Too late! The express was already in the Quintinshill's section. Nothing could stop it now.

Less than a minute after the troop train had slammed into the local, and with flames shooting from the wreckage, the express train smashed into what was left of it. The two engines were heaped on one another, carriages were overturned and telescoped. Men were helplessly pinned beneath them. Fed by gas from the cylinders under the carriages, the flames spread. The carriage doors were jammed closed, trapping those still alive inside an in inferno of scarlet flames and dense smoke.

Someone at the scene heard a soldier plead, 'Shoot me, mate. For God's sake shoot me.' A doctor heard another cry, 'For Christ's sake, get me out,' Crawling under the flaming carriage on which fire hoses were already playing, he found the man pinned by the leg. He had no option but to amputate it there and then.

It took three hours for the

fire brigade to arrive from Carlisle, by which time the heart-breaking task of counting the dead was already underway. Eight people had died in the express and many more were injured. Two passengers on the local had been killed. The driver and the fireman on the troop-train died instantly. A colonel and sergeant who survived the crash took a roll call of the men who were able to stand unaided. 52 answered it. Of the 485 soldiers on the train, 227 had been killed and 246 were injured, many of them seriously.

James Tinsely and George Meakin were both arrested and charged with manslaughter. Tinsely was sentenced to three years in prison and Meakin to eighteen months. When asked how such an accident could have happened, Tinsely said, 'I forgot about the local on the up-line.'

1916

THE SOMME

A black day for the British

In December 1915, just over a year after the first shots in World War One had been fired, Britain, France, Russia and Italy got together at Chantilly and agreed to launch simultaneous offensives on three fronts in the New Year. The plan was a victory for one of the French representatives, General Joseph-Jacques Joffre, Commander-in-Chief of the French Army.

Just before Christmas, the British Commander-in-Chief, Field-Marshall Sir Douglas Haig, held a private meeting with Joffre to discuss tactics. Haig's preference was for a British attack in Flanders: Joffre advocated a joint British-French push along the River Somme, at the point where the British and French lines joined. With the instructions of the Supreme War Council that the driving policy must be the closest co-operation between the French and British, Haig yielded to Joffre.

The original plan was to launch the offensive in July the following year with 25 English divisions attacking north of the Somme and 40 French ones in the south, but the German offensive at Verdun in February of that year changed all that. With the French suffering huge losses, Haig agreed to extend the British share of the front line and brought the date forward to late June, giving him less time than he would have liked to bring his men up to battle fitness.

The revised plan was for the British to put 13 divisions into the attack along 27 kilometres of the front, while the battle-hardened French would order 11 divisions into action along about thirteen kilometres, having previously agreed to launch an offensive over 40 kilometres.

Haig wanted an offensive aimed at capturing targets deep behind the German lines. A former cavalry officer, he was keen to bring his former regiment in at the earliest opportunity. One of his most senior generals, Sir Henry Rawlinson wanted a much more limited attack. Rawlinson wanted to use lengthy artillery bombardment to pound the first line of German trenches and cut the wires (to be achieved by using shrapnel shells, which exploded into a hail of steel balls six metres above the ground) and then consolidate and destroy the inevitable German counter-attack. This would then be repeated in a 'bite and hold' system of attack. As the infantry advanced, the artillery would fire shells ahead of them to prevent the enemy reoccupying their defensive positions. The infantry would then advance again and when they were holding their ground, the artillery would fire ahead of them, preparing the ground for a further infantry push.

In order that the foot soldiers would not get ahead of the artillery, Rawlinson planned to send the infantry in a series of waves at one-minute intervals, the men moving slowly, at around 100 metres every two minutes. And as they would be carrying over 30 kilos of equipment, much of it to be used to fortify positions already conquered for them by the artillery, the soldiers were to be ordered not to run until they were within 20 metres of the enemy trenches.

Haig didn't like Rawlinson's plans. The field-marshal wanted to shorten the length of the artillery bombardment to give the Germans less warning of an attack. He suggested that the infantry should rush the trenches as soon as the bombardment stopped: and he wanted to take the first and second lines of German defences, not just the first one that was Rawlinson's objective.

Rawlinson believed that the British artillery was not heavy enough to carry out his objective in the shortened time that Haig suggested, and that the infantrymen were not well enough trained to do what the Field Marshall wanted them to. Consequently, he rejected Haig's first two suggestions. He compromised on the third, agreeing to make the part of the German second line which was within his guns' range one of the first day's objectives.

The date and time for the infantry to move forward was fixed for June 29, at 07.30. On the early hours of 24 June, 1,500 British field guns, howitzers and mortars began the bombardment. Thanks to the meticulous records that were kept, we know exactly how many shells were fired – 1,508, 652: more than had been used in the first year of the war on all fronts.

For 80 minutes every morning, starting at 06.25 every gun fired as many shells as possible. The bombing continued at a reduced rate for the rest of the day, with half the guns falling silent when night fell.

On the morning when the infantry were to go into the attack, the guns were to stop firing fifteen minutes earlier than on the previous days. The Germans would, it was hoped, be expecting more shelling and be taken by surprise by the attack.

The bombardment was so intense that the guns could be heard in Kent on the other side of the English Channel. But things did not quite go according to plan. It had been hoped that air reconnaissance would be able to locate the German's concrete machine-gun post, telling the British artillery where to direct their fire. But low cloud and drizzle made this impossible.

Things were made worse by the fact that a fairly large proportion (some say 30 per cent) of the shells failed to explode, and the shrapnel shells that were to cut the enemy wires had faulty time fuses and didn't do their job. This was partly due to inexperience on the part of the gunners who set them. And if that wasn't bad enough, there simply weren't enough British guns to do the job that had been asked of them.

Heavy rain during the week made the approach roads, trenches and crater-ridden no-man's-land between the two fronts too wet and muddy to keep up with the strict timetable of advance that had been planned. The infantry offensive was put off until 1 July and the bombardment had to be slackened to ensure that the ammunition would last.

At 07.30 on 1 July, the British guns fell silent as the

Over the top: *the first day of the Somme attack, 1 July 1916, cost the British 20,000 dead*

artillery began to readjust their gunsites to target the second line. Even as they did so, whistles were blown in the British trenches and 66,000 infantrymen poured from them, through the holes that had been cut in their wire into no-man's land and on towards German positions.

But even as infantrymen were climbing the ladders out of the trenches, those in front of them were being mowed down by enemy guns, German lookouts having alerted their comrades as soon as the first British head was spotted coming out of the trenches. And if that wasn't bad enough, the careful co-operation between the British infantry and artillery on which the whole success of the operation depended disintegrated in the fog of war.

On the eve of the battle, Haig wrote, 'The wire has never been so well cut, nor artillery preparations so thorough.' The 21,000 men who were killed or listed as missing that day would hardly have agreed with him.

The Battle of the Somme went on until the third week in November. By then the British, the Commonwealth and Dominions had lost 420,000 men, the French 200,000 and the Germans between 437,000 and 680,000. The 32-kilometre British front had been advanced by less than 10 kilometres – each metre won at the cost of 65 allied lives.

1917

PASSCHENDAELE

Mud, mud, inglorious mud.

Eight months after the Battle of the Somme had cost the lives of over one million men, Field-Marshall Sir Douglas Haig's refusal to listen to advice given him by experts caused thousands more of the men in his command to lose their lives. This time at Passchendaele.

Haig, Commander-in-Chief of the British Expeditionary Force, decided to bombard German positions in Flanders with the biggest artillery barrage so far seen in the war. He ordered the guns to fire, heedless of the warnings he had received from the Belgian government that the low-lying terrain had only been reclaimed from marshlands by generations of hard-working labourers. Already prone to become water-logged, constant bombardment could destroy the delicate balance between the forces of nature and Belgian engineering skills.

Haig turned a deaf ear to the Belgians and to the weather forecast which predicted heavy rain for the time of the planned assault. And on 21 July, 1917 3,091 British guns went into action, pounding the area with 4.25 million shells. Nearly five tonnes of British explosives fell on every square metre of what was to be the battlefield. As the Belgians had feared, the drainage system collapsed and the area was turned into a swamp by the constant, driving rain.

Regardless, Haig ordered thousands of his men into battle. The mud was so thick, waist deep at places, that when soldiers fell over and landed face down, many were unable to get up and hundreds of men drowned in it. From their positions on ridges above the mud, German gunners turned a mud bath into a blood bath.

Back at headquarters, at a safe distance behind the British front line, Haig and his staff-officers studied their maps and charts, and moved their flags and pins around when they received news from the front. Never once did it occur to them to go and see for themselves the quagmire in which thousands of allied soldiers were dying.

1924

WASHINGTON DC

Copy cats

Shortly after his election as President of the United States, President Calvin Coolidge invited some friends from his home state of Vermont to dine at the White House.

Slightly overawed by their surroundings, and unsure or presidential protocol, the men and women copied the president's every move, watching carefully what knife and fork he used for what course and using the corresponding ones in their own place settings, and making sure they drank from the correct glasses.

When coffee was served, President Coolidge poured half of his into his saucer. If the guests were surprised, they didn't show it: they dutifully poured half of the coffee from their cups into their saucers. He added cream to the coffee in his saucer: they added cream to the coffee in their saucers. He added sugar to his coffee and cream: they added sugar to their coffee and cream. He picked up his spoon: the guests picked up their spoons. He stirred the contents of his saucer: his guests stirred the contents of their cups. He picked up his saucer: his guests picked up their saucers. He laid his saucer on the floor for his cat . . .

1928

WASHINGTON DC

An Optimistic Forecast

During an address to the nation in 1928, President Herbert Hoover said, 'We in America today are nearer the final triumph over poverty than ever in the history of the land.' Within twelve months the American stock market collapsed and the clouds of depression loomed over the United States and the rest of the Western world.

1929

NEW YORK

The Wall Street Crash

In the 1920s share prices in the USA rose year after year. Many Americans believed that they could make money easily by investing in shares, and many people bought them, not realising that they could lose all of their money.

Share prices went up because companies encouraged people to go on buying on credit. Hire purchase was easily available, but few people realised that it was very dangerous to go on selling on credit. Eventually people would not be able to make the repayments.

Some companies that people invested their money in were bogus; they simply did not exist. Other companies did not tell the truth. It was difficult for investors to know what they were buying.

The presidents in the 1920s, Warren Harding and Calvin Coolidge, believed that it was not their job to interfere with the markets.

Some Americans predicted that a crash was coming, but very few people took them seriously. Most people believed that the USA was so wealthy and so powerful that it could not happen. They were wrong.

When the crash came, it led to a massive loss of confidence on the part of the millions who had invested on Wall Street. Instead of investing and spending, people now began to save. All over the USA people drew their money out of banks and kept it at home. Many banks collapsed as people withdrew their money and many companies went bankrupt as people stopped spending. Millions of people were thrown out of work and by 1933 13,000,000 people were unemployed: they often lost their homes and were forced out onto the streets. Many began to live in huge shanty-towns on the outskirts of US cities. Here families lived in old crates and shacks put together from orange boxes, and these shanty-towns became known as "Hoovervilles" after President Herbert Hoover, who did little to help the unemployed, believing as he did in "Rugged Individualism". When he eventually offered some help in 1931, it was only in the form of loans.

When ex-servicemen gathered in Washington in August 1932 to ask for their war service bonuses Hoover had them forced away by the army. So when Hoover stood for re-election in November 1932, he was defeated very easily by Franklin Roosevelt.

Britain was also badly affected by the crash. There was extremely high unemployment in the heavy industries such as shipbuilding, coal, steel and textiles. Shipbuilding was very badly hit as orders for new ships dried up. As world trade fell, no new ships were needed. This in turn affected the coal and steel industries, which depended on shipbuilding for many of their orders. Textiles, cotton and wool suffered because India and Japan began to produce these goods more cheaply. Cotton and wool were also affected by the development of man-made fibres, such as dacron and rayon. These were cheaper, easier to wash and longer-lasting. The collapse of these industries led to extreme hardship in the areas of Britain where these industries were concentrated, e.g. south Wales, the north-east around Newcastle and central Scotland, but the best known of all was Jarrow. Here unemployment reached 80 per cent at one point, sparking the Jarrow hunger march to London. And all this because share buyers didn't read the small print!

Thirsty: *the novelist Arnold Bennett, who died after drinking the water in Paris*

1931

PARIS

Water way to go

When English novelist Arnold Bennett (1867–1931) was in Paris, he was told that the water was not safe to drink. 'Nonsense!' exclaimed the author of *Clayhanger, The Card* and other classics, reaching across the table to pour himself a glass from a carafe. Two months later he died from the cholera he caught a result of his defiant gesture.

1932

LONDON

A jewel of a find

After a busy day's Christmas shopping in the West End, a London couple (history does not record their names) clambered into a taxi, laid their purchases on the seat beside them and on the floor at their feet, and told the driver to head for home. Once there, the found that they had one parcel more than they had bought. When they unwrapped it, they found a jewel case containing a king's ransom in emeralds and rubies.

Good citizens, the couple took their find to the police who expected it to be claimed within hours. When three days later when no one had come forward, the police started to make enquiries and traced the jewels to a woman who had not even realized that she had mislaid the gems.

She was the Grand Duchess Zenia Romanova who had escaped from Bolshevik Russia fourteen years earlier. And the emeralds and rubies literally were worth a king's ransom – they were part of the Russian Crown Jewels.

1934

LINCOLNSHIRE

A little knowledge is a fatal thing

When she was a young woman, Ethel Major made the same mistake that countless other girls have before and after. The dressmaker daughter of a Lincolnshire gamekeeper, Ethel had believed the young man she was courting when he had said he loved her and that he would marry her when the war was over, as it was likely that he would soon be called to the front. In the meantime . . . Nine months later, in 1915, she gave birth to an illegitimate daughter that her parents brought up as their own child.

Three years later, Ethel married Arthur Major, a van driver, and the year after that they had their first baby. Unable to afford a house of their own, the Majors stayed with Ethel's parents until they had scraped enough money together. It took them ten years before they had enough to move out – to the village of Kirby on Bain. They took Ethel's 'sister' with them, and it wasn't long before tongues were wagging. It wasn't long, either, before Arthur put two and two together and came up with the right answer, for Ethel had never told him about her first baby.

The marriage, never especially on an even keel, began to go seriously downhill. Arthur was understandably angry, and his anger turned to fury when his wife refused to tell him who the father was. For all Arthur knew it could be any man in the area. He started to drink heavily and became increasingly violent towards Ethel. Although she was a strong-willed woman, Ethel kept all this to herself, until she found out that her husband was seeing another woman. That was too much for her and she presented him with an ultimatum: either stop seeing her, or Ethel would tell the world that he was a drunken bully and wife beater. He responded by saying he was about to place an advertisement in the *Horncastle News* saying that he would no longer accept any responsibility for his wife's debts.

The advert was booked to appear in the newspaper on 26 May, 1934. Four days before that, Arthur was taken ill with severe stomach pains and convulsions. He also started foaming at the mouth. Ethel put everything down to some corned beef he had eaten. He died two days later.

As soon as she had cancelled the advert in the Horncastle News, Ethel started to arrange the funeral. But even as friends and neighbours were gathering at the house, a policeman called to say that the coroner had ordered that it would have to be postponed.

It turned out that the police had received an anonymous letter, claiming that a neighbour's dog had died after eating scraps of food thrown out by Ethel Major. One of Arthur's workmates then recalled that he had seen a bird die after pecking at one of the sandwiches Ethel had prepared for Arthur's lunch one day not so far back.

The dog's body was exhumed and the post-mortem that was carried out on it showed that it had indeed been poisoned. And when a post-mortem was held on Arthur, it, too, showed that he had died of poisoning.

When confronted with the news, Ethel said, 'I did not know my husband died of strychnine poisoning.' At which point, in true B-movie manner, a detective said, 'No one mentioned strychnine, Mrs Major.' for that fact was known only to the police and the pathologist who had carried out the inquest.

'Oh,' said Ethel Major. 'I'm so sorry. I must have made a mistake.'

The police were convinced that she had made no such error, but before they could even think of charging her with Arthur's murder, they had to find out how she could have got her hands on strychnine. It was, still is, virtually impossible to buy without signing the poison book – and no chemist recalled Ethel or anyone resembling her trying to buy it.

Among the few people who can obtain it legally are gamekeepers who use it to get rid of vermin. Police inquiries showed that Ethel's father had some, but he kept it in a locked box to which he had the only key. There had been a second one, but that had been lost ten years before Arthur's death. When it was found at the bottom of Ethel's handbag, she was charged with her husband's murder.

At her trial at Lincoln Assizes she was defended by Norman Birkett, a lawyer whose powers of advocacy had never failed to secure the release of any murderer he had defended. No witnesses were called on Ethel's behalf and nor did she take the stand. No doubt, given that Ethel was obviously what we have come to call a 'battered wife' the courts would have treated her with some sympathy. But this was seventy years ago. Birkett's oratory failed and Ethel Major was hanged at Hull Prison just before Christmas in 1934.

Had she not mentioned strychnine, had she thrown away the key to her father's poison box, the evidence against her would have been circumstantial and she would probably never have been charged. She paid for these two mistakes with her life.

1938

NEW YORK

A slight navigation error

The fog was thickening at the airfield near New York where pilot Douglas Corrigan was filling his plane's fuel tank, ready for a flight to California. An experienced flier, Corrigan had complete faith in his abilities to pilot his aircraft through the fog. And so, his tanks full he climbed into the cockpit and took off. Twenty-eight hours later, having lost his bearings thanks to the fog he landed – in Ireland.

1940s

LONDON

His Majesty was amused

In 1940, with the German armies seemingly unstoppable in Europe, King Haakon of Norway and his family came to Britain from where he regularly broadcast to his people at home.

On one of the first occasions when he did so, he turned up at the BBC's studios in London to record a message, which was to start with the deep and serious voice of a BBC announcer saying, 'This is London.' The words were to be heralded with a royal fanfare.

Unfortunately, in classic Chinese Whispers manner, the request to the BBC Sound Library was taken down by the telephonist there as, '. . . supply music for a funfair.'

The King took his place at the microphone. The announcer spoke the words, by now familiar all over occupied Europe to those listening on illicit radio sets, which were followed by barrel organ music with the voice of a barker shouting, 'Roll up! Roll up! All the fun of the fair'.

1941

HOLLYWOOD

A fatal stumble

During the filming of *They Died With Their Boots On*, a Hollywood version of the Battle of Little Bighorn, an actor called Bill Mead was taking part in one of the celluloid cavalry charges when his horse stumbled. Afraid that he would fall on his sword, he made the mistake of throwing it ahead of him. Unfortunately, it landed hilt down and when Mead fell off his horse, he impaled himself on the blade.

1941

HAWAII

They were warned

7 December 1941 is a date that was described by President Roosevelt as one that 'will live in infamy'. It was the day when almost 400 planes swept out of the sky above Pearl Harbor, devastated the American fleet and killed over 2,400 civilians and US servicemen. But had the Americans paid any heed to the warnings, the damage would have been much less and probably half that number would have survived.

By late 1941, war had been raging in Europe and other parts of the world for over two years. The Americans had kept out of the conflict, but the Japanese were determined to bring them into it, and to do so in a way that would inflict maximum damage.

The first warnings that something was afoot came in mid-November when American agents in Japan reported that Japanese Navy ships were slipping out of their home ports and were assembling in Tankan Bay, in the north of the country. On 26 November the nine destroyers, eight tankers, six aircraft carriers, three cruisers, three submarines and two battleships sailed into the Pacific, to join the fleet of 25 submarines, five of them carrying midget submarines, had sailed from the area a few days before.

The Japanese were so keen to maintain the element of surprise that was essential to their plans, that as the huge fleet steamed to its destination, halfway across the Pacific, it had been ordered to maintain radio silence. No refuse was to be dumped overboard, low-smoke fuel was used and at night a strict blackout was enforced. Meanwhile, back in home waters, Japanese ships raised the level of radio communications several fold to convince eavesdropping US agents that the full Japanese fleet was still at home.

Five days after the ships sailed, Vice-Admiral Chuichi Nagamo heard the strange message that was broadcast from Tokyo: 'Climb Mount Niitaka'. He was the only man in the fleet who knew what it meant. Japanese Supreme Command had decided to go ahead with their plan to bring the United States into the war by bombing the American Pacific Fleet at its base at Pearl Harbor on the Hawaiian island of Oahu.

Nagamo had been ordered that if his ships were spotted at any time on or before 6 December, the Americans would know something big was up, the surprise element would have been lost and he was to turn back. Otherwise the attack was go ahead as planned – at 08.00 on 7 December.

The Americans were well aware that the Japanese were planning war. US agents had broken the code they used when sending messages between Tokyo and the Japanese embassy in Washington. One of the transmissions had been a long declaration the final part of which stated that the Japan was now at war with the United States. But the

Americans believed that when the attack came, it would be in the Far East, Borneo perhaps, or the Philippines.

On 5 December, three weeks after US agents had reported that the vast fleet was amassing in Tankan Bay, the FBI tapped into a conversation between Tokyo and a Japanese dentist in Hawaii, one of the large Japanese community there. The two men talked about the number of ships and aircraft in and around Pearl Harbor, the island's defences and flowers! The eavesdroppers were well aware that references to the island's flora were some sort of code, but they had no idea what they meant. And the final words, 'The hibiscus and poinsettia are now in bloom,' had them baffled. If it was a coded reference to an imminent attack, it could hardly be in Hawaii, the Americans reasoned: it was well out of reach of Japanese bombers and fighter aircraft.

Saturday night was party night in Hawaii for the US personnel posted there. And even as the servicemen were drinking and dancing in the islands' bars and clubs, Japanese submarines were closing in on Pearl Harbor. Their crews' orders were to torpedo any US ships that tried to sail from their berths once the airborne attack was launched a few hours later. Simultaneously with the fighter attack, mini-submarines from five of the Japanese U-boats were to fire their twin torpedoes against the warships from inside the harbour.

At 03.30 the US minesweeper *Condor*, on patrol in the coastal waters around the island, spotted a submarine periscope that seemed to heading for Pearl Harbor. A signal was sent to the destroyer *Ward* and battle stations were called and held. But after an hour when there was no further sign of any submarine, they were called off.

An hour and a half after spotting the periscope trail, *Condor* went off duty. As she approached the harbour, the anti-submarine net was drawn back to allow her to enter. Because other ships were expected to be sailing in and out of the harbour over the next few hours, the net was not closed again. It would have been closed had either *Condor* or *Ward* reported that there was a submarine in the area. But they failed to do so, and the Japanese mini-submarines slipped through and bided their time.

Even as *Condor* went steaming into harbour, 400 kilometres north of the island the Japanese were putting the finishing touches to their preparations. Six aircraft carriers with over 400 planes aboard were in position, waiting for the signal to go. The Japanese planned to launch two strikes using 350 planes, each loaded with bombs and torpedoes. The other aircraft on deck were either reserves or were to be used to defend the fleet and for reconnaissance.

At 06.00, just as dawn was breaking, the first wave of planes took off, the roar of their engines drowning the cheers of the carrier crews that lined the decks.

Forty-five minutes later, *Ward*, still patrolling the waters around the entrance to Pearl Harbor, spotted a mini-submarine. Moments later, American guns were pounding the enemy boat, before the captain gave the order to run at it and drop depth charges. They hit true and the Japanese craft was destroyed. Fifteen minutes later, a second mini-sub came into *Ward's* gunsites and the same tactics were used to blast it out of the water.

At seven o'clock, the second wave of Japanese planes was waved off from the fleet of aircraft carriers, and headed south in the tail streams of their compatriots.

Meanwhile, *Ward* had radioed two coded messages of the events of the previous fifteen minutes back to base. Unfortunately, the US decoding capabilities were not up to scratch and it was not until 07.15 that the first message reached Lieutenant-Commander Harold Kaminsky, a veteran reservist and then only man on duty at US Naval Headquarters in Pearl Harbor. He immediately started to call senior naval officers in their homes. Many of them were in bed sound asleep and when the phones by their bedsides started to ring, they no doubt started to curse themselves for having partied so hard the night before.

On the ships in harbour, morning colours were being hoisted and the men on duty busied themselves with their usual duties, quite unaware that within a few minutes all hell was about to be let loose.

Fifteen minutes before Kaminsky received the first of *Ward's* signals, radar screens at the US Army station on Oahu picked up two blips – most likely two Japanese reconnaissance planes at the head of the first wave of enemy aircraft. The information was passed on to Oahu's military information centre to be plotted and assessed, but no immediate action was taken. It seems that just as in Britain, in the words of the Jack Buchanan song at four o'clock everything stops for tea, at Pearl Harbor at seven o'clock on 7 December, 1941, everything stopped for breakfast.

Among those looking forward to their coffee and eggs were the men just about to go off duty at the Opana radar station on the north of Oahu. A few minutes after 7.00 they picked up the first signs of the huge bank of aircraft heading towards the island. They immediately radioed the information centre. But there was only the switchboard operator and one officer on duty, and both of them were looking forward to their breakfasts. Thinking that their signals were being ignored, the men at Opana packed up and went to their mess rooms for coffee and whatever was on the menu.

A few minutes later, the Japanese planes were approaching the coast while on board the battleship *Nevada* in Pearl Harbour, the bandsmen and crew were getting ready for the ceremony that accompanied the hoisting of the colours.

It was 7.55 and the strains of *The Star Spangled Banner* were floating over the Harbor from the *Nevada's* decks when the first plane attacked. As it approached the battleship, the crew must have been able to see the torpedo that dropped from the Japanese plane. His payload delivered, the pilot took his plane low over the *Nevada*, machine-gun fire blazing from the rear. The bullets tore the US flag to shreds, but the band manfully played on and finished the tune they were playing before running for cover.

Within five minutes the message, 'Air Raid on Pearl Harbor – this is no drill' had been received in Washington and every ship in the US Pacific and Atlantic fleets.

Between then and 10.00am wave after wave of Japanese

Devastation: *the Japanese surprise attack on Pearl Harbor sank 13 US Navy ships and left 2400 dead*

aircraft swept over Pearl Harbor and the surrounding air bases, dropping their deadly bombs and torpedoes.

A cloud of thick, acrid black smoke shrouded the Harbor as oil from the damaged ships spilled from their tanks and caught fire. The battleship *Oklahoma*, blasted by five torpedoes, capsized. A Japanese bomb scored a direct hit on her sister battleship *Arizona*, which sank to the bottom of the Harbor, taking 1,100 men with her. The battleship *West Virginia* took the full impact of six torpedoes and met the same fate as *Arizona*, but she was later salvaged along with her sister battleships *California*, which had been hit by two torpedoes, and *Nevada*. *Nevada* was hit by a torpedo and two bombs but was still able to try and make a run for the open sea. Unfortunately she ran aground. Among the other battleships that were damaged but repairable were *Tennessee, Pennsylvania* and *Maryland*.

Utah, a target ship, and *Helena*, a cruiser, were both hit by torpedoes and sunk. The same torpedo that hit *Helena* sank the minelayer *Oglala*. The cruiser *Raleigh* managed to stay afloat after being holed, but in the Harbor's dry dock, the destroyer *Shaw* exploded, while her sister ships *Cassin* and *Downes* were totally destroyed by enemy bombs.

Honolulu, a US cruiser, was put out of action, and 13 kilometres away the city that had given the ship her name also suffered some damage-from one Japanese bomb and 40-odd US shells fired at the enemy aircraft overhead by ships in the city's harbour.

The Japanese losses were minimal by comparison to the Americans' – 30 aircraft and five mini-submarines. The US lost just over 2,400 men and women, including 68 civilians and the men who drowned when *Arizona* sank.

Five hours after the attack, a cable from Washington was received by the commander of US ground forces in Hawaii, Lieutenant-General Walter C. Short. It read that the Japanese were planning to present an official declaration in Washington that morning, at 7.30 Honolulu time. The last sentence read, 'Just what significance the hour may have we do not know – but be on the alert.'

The cable had been received on the island 22 minutes before the first Japanese plane attacked Nevada. It had taken five-and-a-half hours to reach the General not just because of the attack itself, but because of a delay at the decoding centre, it being a Sunday!

Had US Intelligence acted on the reports that the Japanese were amassing a huge fleet in Tankan Bay in mid-November, then perhaps Japanese cover might have been blown and the attack called off (no doubt, the Japanese would then have provoked the US into the War by attacking American installations somewhere else).

But given that the attack did go ahead at Pearl Harbor, if the early warnings that Japanese planes were approaching the island has been heeded, then perhaps the US would not have sustained such heavy costs both in the ships that were lost or damaged and in the 2,403 people who were killed.

1942

QUEBEC

Flying on thin ice

During World War II, Harry Griffith of the US Air Force was co-pilot of a Boston bomber. While others in the service were seeing action in other parts of the world, Griffin was still in North America, doing routine training flights over Quebec.

On this particular day in December, 1942 he was in his seat by the pilot, the only other person on board, as the plane flew over Lake St Louis in Quebec. When it came to the point of the flight when he had to check the bomb bay, Griffith clambered into the cramped compartment, failing to notice the bomb-bay doors had not been closed properly.

Unable to stop himself, he slipped through them. Somehow, he managed to grab the edge of one of the doors and as he clutched it for dear life, he yelled for help. The pilot, Sid Gerow, a 29-year-old from Minnesota, heard his co-pilot's screams but couldn't leave the controls to drag him back in. All he could do was circle the frozen lake, getting lower an lower until the plane was skimming through the air just above it at 160km/h: any slower and the engines would have stalled.

When the plane was seven or eight metres above the lake, Griffith let go his grip and dropped onto the ice, rolling over and over it for three or four hundred metres until he came to a crashing stop in the snow banked thickly on the banks of the lake.

After radioing for a rescue team, Gerow took his plane back to base. It wasn't long before a local farmer found Griffith, sitting in the snow, suffering from a few cuts and bruises and vowing that whoever had left the bomb-bay doors opened wouldn't make the same mistake twice.

1946

HECHINGEN, GERMANY

Soup to die for

This may sound like an urban myth, but Bill Bryson, Jnr, the best-selling travel book writer, swears that this story is true. In the months after the Second World War came to an end, life was grim in Germany. Food was scarce and many families came to depend of food parcels from relatives in the United States. Among these families was the Wallishausers who lived in the small town of Hechingen in what was then West Germany. In one of the parcels they received was an unlabelled tin which when it was opened contained what

Frau Wallishauser assumed to be powdered soup. Adding a little semolina to give it body, she duly cooked it and served it to her family. Delicious, they said. They best soup they had tasted since before the war. A few days later, the Wallishausers received a letter from their cousins saying that they hoped the parcel had been received for it contained a small can filled with the ashes of their late grandmother whose dying wish was that her remains be buried in German soil.

1946

HOLLYWOOD

A few wonderful mistakes

Frank Capra's movie, *It's a Wonderful Life*, is generally regarded as one of the most perfect and heartwarming movies ever made. Heartwarming certainly. Perfect? Well in the first scene, when George finds his brother's grave, the year he died, 1919, is clear to see. The next time he sees it, it's obscured by snow and George has to dig it out to find out when his brother died. Later, when George and Mary are getting ready to drive Martini's family to their new home, there's a close-up of Mary holding the goat's horn. Cut to a long shot and she's got both arms around the girl in her lap. And towards the end of the movie, George had a Christmas wreath on his arm when he enters the Loan Company building. When he's told there's a phone call, he tosses the wreath on a table and picks up the phone. In the next shot, the wreath is back on his arm.

The film was not the first in which there was the odd error. And it certainly wasn't the last . . .

Back to the Future: When Marty, the character that made Michael J Fox's name, goes to Hill Valley High it's 1955. The music he hears is *Mr Sandman* – a song that wasn't released until 1958.

Braveheart: Mel Gibson's box-office blockbuster in which he tinkered just a little with history (did William Wallace really have an affair with Edward II's queen?) stirred the nationalist heart of many a Scot. But surely someone should have noticed the white van that makes an unscheduled appearance in the distant background in one scene.

Castaway: Apart from the fact that had the plane crash which results in Tom Hanks being marooned on a desert island couldn't have happened as it was shown (the plane would have flipped forward and Hanks would have exited upside down) he undergoes an unscripted change of name. For most of the film his character is called, Chuck.' But as he pulls out of his girlfriend's driveway near the end of the movie, she calls out, 'Jack! Jack! Jack!'

Commando: Before Arnold Schwartzenieger clambers into a yellow Porsche, the car is badly dented right down the left side. But when our hero gets into it, it's miraculously perfect.

Forest Gump: Another memorable performance from Tom Hanks: another couple of boobs (one strictly for whatever is the cinema equivalent of anorak). When the eponymous hero gets his discharge papers, he's standing on a three-point shot line, an innovation introduced in 1984, many years after the event. And when he says that one of the characters, Jenny, died on a Saturday, he seems to overlook the fact that her gravestone says she passed away on 22 March, 1982 – a Monday.

Gladiator: Russell Crowe deserved the praise which was heaped on him for his brilliant performance in a brilliant movie, but there was one anachronism that deserved its own Oscar. In one scene, printed handouts are being distributed promoting the big fight – at least a thousand years before the European invention of the printing press. Another booboo occurs the morning after the battle with the Germans, when Maximus gives one of the horses a piece of apple. Just for a

You dirty rat: *the 'immortal' line never actually spoken by James Cagney*

second someone appears between our hero and the horse: it's one of the crew wearing a pair of blue Levis! And a third one is in one of the battle scenes when a chariot overturns: once the dust settles, spot the gas canister in the back of the chariot!

Harry Potter and the Philosopher's Stone: At the start of term when Harry has moved into Gryffindor, he goes to the feast and sits down next to Ron to wait for the food. When it appears, Harry has mysteriously moved to the other side of the table and is sitting next to Hermione. Later in the movie, when the three friends run to Hagrid after their end-of-term exams, one of the lines Harry has to say ends, 'Why didn't I see it before?' Watch closely and you'll see Hermione mouthing them in the background. And during that fantastic game of Quidditch, in one scene Hermoine's hair is crimped. Later, after Neville has fallen off his broomstick, her red mane is straight and a few seconds after that, she's wearing her hair crimped again. And when Fluffy wakes he dribbles all over Ron. Seconds later when he and Harry and Hermoine fall into the Devil's Snare, Ron's shirt looks to be as dry as a bone. And one more for luck. During the Sorting Ceremony, Susan Bones, the girl with the lovely, long curly hair is assigned to Hufflepuff House. Later, when the trainee witches and wizards from Gryffindor and Slytherin are sitting in Professor Snape's Potion class who is there when she should have been somewhere else? Susan Bones, the girl with the lovely, long hair!

Independence Day: One of the shots on the Moon shows

the flag left behind by the crew of Apollo 11 after their historic landing in 1969. Unfortunately when the Eagle took off to rendezvous with the orbiting capsule, the blast knocked the flag over.

Raiders of the Lost Ark: Remember the bit where Indiana Jones aka Harrison Ford falls into the Well of Souls and comes to face to fang with a cobra? If you look closely enough, you can see the snake's reflection on the dividing glass that's not supposed to be there. Not only that, there are smudged fingerprints on the glass, too.

Spider Man: When Peter shoots his web at the lamp on the bedroom dresser, it falls against the wall and smashes. Moments later when Aunt Mary is talking to Peter from the bedroom door, the lamp is on the dresser, as good as new. And remember the scene where our hero, comes to the rescue of Mary Jane when she is being mugged by four villains? Spider Man despatches two of them by throwing them into a window behind her. In the next frame Spider Man is giving the other two men what for, before the camera pans to Mary Jane, who just happens to be standing in front of the window, which has been miraculously repaired in the space of a couple of seconds.

Zulu: The celluloid version of the Battle of Rorke's Drift, the heroic defence put up by handful of Welsh Guards against native warriors during the 1879 Zulu War was stirring stuff, but someone should have told several of the actors that Rolex wristwatches weren't around then.

1950

LONDON

A serious miscarriage of justice

Throughout history, many men and women have been found guilty of murder and executed for their crimes, only for evidence to be uncovered after the event that cast doubt on their convictions. One of the most famous of such cases was that of Timothy John Evans who was executed in Pentonville Prison on 9 March, 1950 . . .

Less than four months before he was hanged, Evans walked into the police station at Merthyr Tydfil in South Wales. The officers on duty noticed that he looked more than a little frightened and was obviously unsure of himself. Small wonder, for a few minutes later, he confessed to the murder of his wife.

Evans was a local man, ill-educated and not particularly intelligent. He had left Wales a few years before and had settled to London where he lived in the top floor of a seedy house in Rillington Place, a shabby street in the west of the city, with his wife Beryl and his baby daughter, Geraldine.

The couple had a volatile relationship not helped by their struggle to survive on Evans' meagre wages as a van driver. There were violent rows when Beryl told him that she was expecting their second child. The arguments were not just because he knew that the money he earned would simply not stretch to feed another mouth, but because Beryl said that she had no intention of having the baby.

Evans, as he later told the police, had been against the proposed abortion, but Beryl was adamant. She was going to have the pregnancy terminated, and if she couldn't find someone to do it for her, she would do the job herself.

Evans told the Merthyr police that one day in early November, 1949, he had stopped off at a transport café when he was on his way home from work. He claimed that he fell into conversation with a man in the café who, when he heard Evans' tale of woe, gave him a bottle of liquid, which, the stranger said, would bring about a miscarriage.

According to Evans, he took the bottle, even though he was still against the abortion, but when he returned to Rillington Place, Beryl saw it in his jacket pocket. When she found out what it was, she told him that she was going to bring her pregnancy to an end the next day.

Evans went on to say that that when he got home the next day, he found that Beryl was dead. Something had obviously gone wrong with her abortion. In the early hours of the following morning, 8 November, he had carried her body down the stairs, heaved off a manhole cover over a drain outside the house and dumped Beryl's body into the hole. Later, he had quit his job, sold his furniture and headed to an aunt's house in Wales.

As soon as they had taken Evans' statement, the Merthyr Tydfil police telephoned the Metropolitan Police in London. When they arrived at Rillington Place, the found the manhole, but the policeman who tried to move it could not shift the heavy metal disc and had to call for help. In the end it took four burly officers to lift the cover, something that Evans, a frail, slight man, had claimed to have done by himself.

There was no body to be found, although on making inquiries, the police learned that no one had seen or heard anything of either Beryl or baby Geraldine since Evans had left London.

When the news that there was no body beneath the manhole cover was broken to Evans, he changed his story. The new one did not mention either the stranger in the transport café or the bottle. According to this version of events, Evans said that he had told a neighbour, John Christie, who lived in a lower flat at No 10, that Beryl was pregnant but didn't want to have the baby. Christie, Evans said, had offered to help to arrange the abortion.

When Evans had returned from work on the day the abortion was to have taken place, he found Beryl's body, laid out on the bed and covered with an eiderdown. There was blood around her nose and mouth and staining on the eiderdown where it covered the space between her thighs. Christie, Evans told police, had said that the abortion had gone wrong, and that if anyone found out what had happened, they would both go to prison. Evans had said he needed time to think and Christie had left him in the kitchen. When Christie came back, he told Evans that he had put Beryl's body in the vacant first-floor flat and that he would get rid of it after dark. And as for Geraldine, Evans said that Christie had told him that he found a couple in East Acton who were looking after her.

Evans's new story was sent down the line to London and Christie was taken in for questioning. By the time he had arrived at Scotland Yard, police had found the bodies of both Beryl and her baby daughter, wrapped in a green tablecloth and hidden behind a pile of wood in a wash-house in the back garden of the house. Both had been strangled, the baby by a tie that was so tightly knotted it had to be cut from around her neck.

Evans, by now completely bewildered and confused, changed his story yet again, and it was this version that sent him to his death. He told the police that Beryl had got them into debt and that on 8 November, after a furious argument about money, he had lost his temper and strangled her with a piece or rope. Later that night, he had taken her to the first floor flat which he knew to be empty. Two days later, on 10 November, when he got home from work, he had strangled his fourteen-month-old baby with his tie, taken the body downstairs and hidden it, along with Beryl's, in the wash-house where they were later found.

It was customary in the early 1950s that when someone was suspected of multiple murder, they were only charged with one of them – the one that police were certain would lead to conviction. The Metropolitan Police knew that if they charged Evans with Beryl's murder, a skilled lawyer would advise him to plead not guilty to murder but guilty to manslaughter – a non-capital offence. No such plea would be countenanced from someone charged with the murder of a fourteen-month-old baby. So the police charged Timothy Evans with the murder of his daughter.

His trial started on 11 January, 1950 at the Old Bailey before Mr Justice Lewis, who heard Evans retract his confession and blame Christie for both murders. Called to the box, Christie proved to be a very credible witness and two days after the trial began, Timothy Evans was found guilty. After hearing the jury's verdict, the judge donned the black cap and pronounced the death sentence. It was carried out eight weeks later on Tuesday, 9 March.

And there matters may have rested had it not been for the fact that three years after Timothy Evans had been hanged, a new tenant in 10 Rillington Place decided to do a little DIY . . .

It was in March 1953 that Beresford Brown started to fix a bracket to one of the walls in his first-floor flat. As he tapped the wall in one place it sounded hollow. He stripped away a piece of wallpaper to see what was there and found a boarded-up alcove. When he shone a torch into it, the beam fell on the naked body of a dead woman.

When the police arrived, they found two more corpses. The women were later identified as Rita Nelson, Kathleen Maloney and Hectorina MacLellan – all three of them prostitutes and all three strangled by some sort of ligature. Later, another body was found under the floorboards in the front room of the flat. It was Ethel Christie, John Christie's wife. And she, too, had been strangled.

As the search for Christie got underway, police started

digging in the garden where they unearthed two skeletons. They were later identified as Ruth Fuerst and Muriel Eady. They had obviously had been there for some time.

Christie was arrested on Putney Bridge a few days later and admitted that he was responsible for all six deaths. He had killed Ruth Fuerst, who worked as a munitions worker in Mayfair, in 1943, strangling her while they made love one night when his wife was away from home. He had hidden her body under the floorboards of his front room and later buried her in the garden.

Muriel Eady he had killed the following year. She had visited Rillington Place with her boyfriend several times, but one night in October 1944 she visited Christie by herself. When he saw that she had a bad cold, he told her he knew something that would clear her head – inhaling Friar's Balsam bubbled through household gas. The woman was rendered unconscious, then strangled, sexually assaulted and buried alongside Ruth Fuerst. Some months later, when Ruth's skull somehow came to the surface, Christie callously threw it into the shell of a bombed house in nearby St Mark's Gardens, where he knew it would be assumed to belong to an unnamed victim of the Blitz.

In December 1952, Christie murdered his wife Ethel and hid her body under the floorboards of the front room of the first-floor flat. The next three victims all met the same fate as Muriel Eady – gassed with the mixture of Friar's Balsam and household gas, strangled then sexually assaulted after they were dead.

While he was in custody, Christie confessed to another

Evil: *callous Christie, serial killer, is led away by police*

killing – Beryl Evans. Although Evans had been hanged officially for the murder of his baby, Geraldine, it had been taken for granted by judge and jury that he had killed his wife too, although he had never been charged with the crime.

Christie's plea of insanity fell on deaf ears. He was hanged at the same prison and by the same man, Albert Pierrepoint, as Evans had been three years before.

The case caused an outcry. Evans had been convicted partly on the evidence of a man who it turned out had already murdered two women and was to go on to murder four more women at 10 Rillington Place. Now the public were being asked to believe that there had been two murderers living at the same house at the same time, one of whom had murdered seven women, the other the baby of one of them.

There were those who claimed that Christie had only confessed to Beryl Evan's murder to add to his tally of killings. This would, he hoped, increase the chances that his plea of insanity would be successful and that he would escape the hangman. Others were certain that there had been a miscarriage of justice and that when Evans had gone to the gallows, an innocent man was hanged.

As the result of public pressure, including a best-selling book, *10 Rillington Place*, a public inquiry chaired by Mr Justice Brabin was established. The result, though, was not everything that Evans' supporters had wanted. The Brabin Report concluded that Evans may well have murdered his wife, but that Christie had killed Geraldine (something he had always denied), the crime for which Evans had been charged and hanged.

In 1965, Timothy Evans was granted a posthumous free pardon.

It has never been established if one murderer or two lived in Rillington Place, now long since demolished and rebuilt as Ruston Mews, on the fringes of London's fashionable Notting Hill. But that there was a serious miscarriage of justice is beyond doubt, for no jury would have convicted Timothy Evans knowing what was subsequently known about John Christie.

The case added weight to the arguments of those opposed to the death penalty in the United Kingdom and in 1965 capital punishment for murder was abolished. No such mistake could be made again.

1952

GERMANY

The Hollow Sun

Sir William Herschel (1738 – 1822) was one of the most famous astrologers of all time. He discovered the planet Uranus as well as two of its satellites and two of Saturn's moons. He was also convinced that while the surface of the Sun was undoubtedly hot, there was probably a temperate land beneath it where intelligent beings lived. And for some reason he also believed that the social structure of their society was almost identical to that in nineteenth-century Europe.

One would have thought that the idea of a hollow sun would have fizzled out with him. Not so. In 1952 German Godfried Buren proved to his own satisfaction that the Sun was hollow and that within it was a cool globe which is covered with water and hence appears dark. What other people believe to be sunspots, were, according to Buren, holes in the surface through which the dark water was visible.

Buren was so convinced that he was right, that he made the mistake of offering a prize of DM25,000 (about £2,000 in the early 1950s) to anyone who could prove him wrong. The German Astrological Society picked up the gauntlet and did just that.

Buren claimed that what the Society had said was nonsense and refused to pay up. When the German courts found for the Society and ordered him to pay up, he had no alternative but to hand over the money. He went to his grave convinced that he was right, though.

1952

LONDON

Wet! Wet! Wet!

When King George VI died in February, 1952, it was not long after his state funeral that discrete preparations began for the Coronation of his daughter, Queen Elizabeth II. The event could not take place until after a period of official mourning and the decision was taken that the Queen should be crowned in June the following year.

Britain, as the head of the largest empire the world has ever known, was expected to put on a stunning display of pageantry. Kings and queens and heads of states were expected to arrive in London and travel to Westminster Abbey in an open carriage procession to witness the moment when the young queen was crowned.

Anxious about the hundreds of thousands of spectators expected to line the route from Buckingham Palace to the Abbey, the

Royalty in the rain: *the coronation of Queen Elizabeth II goes ahead despite the downpour*

organizers asked the experts to select a date when they could confidently predict fine weather. Records showed that, if the records were anything to go by, there was little chance of rain falling on London on June 2.

June 2 started off wet in London. The rain continued throughout the day and only stopped falling long after Elizabeth had been crowned and anointed as Queen.

1950S

LONDON

A nose for the job

Kay Kendall was one of the most gifted and sophisticated light comedy actresses of the 1950s and early 1960s. Like many other actresses before and after her, she decided that a little cosmetic surgery would improve her looks and career prospects. She went to Sir Archibald McIndoe, one of the most eminent cosmetic surgeons of his day, and asked him to give her a 'Greek'-style nose – the fashionable ideal of the day.

Sir Archibald did as he was bid, but when the bandages were removed from around the actress's face and the swelling had gone down, he was horrified to see that he made a terrible mistake. Far from the straight, dignified nose he had been aiming for, the actress had a tip-tilted, snub nose that was generally despised at the time.

Expecting Ms Kendall to throw one of the tantrums for which she was rapidly becoming famous, Sir Archibald was more that a little relieved when his offer of redoing the job was rejected. Realizing that her new look gave her an air of insouciant sophistication, the actress insisted on keeping it.

Kendall's new nose set a fashion for retrousse noses that lasted into the 1980s. McIndoe's mistake turned out to be a triumph.

1957

GERMANY

The launch of a tragedy

Thalidomide was originally developed after World War II as a sleeping pill to replace the widely prescribed barbiturates, which although effective had two serious faults – they were addictive, and they were dangerous if the person taking them accidentally overdosed. The drug, according to its makers, had neither of these drawbacks and it had the added benefit of soothing the stomach, something that would be of great benefit to women in the early stages of pregnancy who were prone to morning sickness.

The drug is a compound derived from two acids, glutamic, which is one of the amino acids that make up protein, and pthalic, which is a derivative of benzine. Research into producing thalidomide began in Germany in the early 1950s and it was launched there by the pharmaceutical manufacturer Chemie Grunenthal, in 1957 under the brand name Contergan,

Chemie Grunenthal subjected the drug to many laboratory tests to ensure that it had no serious side effects. One test did show that the drug was lethal to cats and dogs if administered in very high doses. This was no great cause for concern: give a hippopotamus enough Aspirin and they will kill it. Another of the tests was to inject the drug into pregnant mice and rats: and when they produced healthy offspring, it was assumed that it could safely be prescribed for pregnant women. Subsequent tests were to show that the animals on which the drug had been tested in the Chemie Grunenthal laboratories did not metabolize it in the same way that humans do. When it was given to pregnant monkeys and rabbits, several of the young to which they gave birth, showed missing or stunted limbs. But these tests were not carried out until after the event . . .

It was the fact that it was thought that the drug could be safely given to pregnant women that caused thalidomide eventually to be prescribed widely in Germany, the United Kingdom, Japan and Australia to women in the first stages of pregnancy when morning sickness is commonly experienced.

In 1959, Chemie Grunenthal received a letter from a German physician, a Dr Voss, reporting that several of the people to whom he had prescribed the drug were suffering side effects including peripheral neuritis, or nerve damage. The letter was the first of several similar ones sent to the company, but in replying to each of them Grunenthal implied that there had been no previous evidence that the drug was potentially dangerous

However, in July 1961, the company were forced to acknowledge that such a link did exist when it paid a Dusseldorf minister, Dr Kersten Thiele, DM750 (around £150) in recognition that the drug they manufactured had, indeed, caused, nerve damage. Despite this, the company continued to manufacture the drug and promote its positive effects. It was also alleged that the company would stop at nothing to silence anyone who tried to say anything against their drug and were even accused of using private detectives to dig up damaging information, which could be used to blacken the reputations of those who complained. It was later alleged that the company suppressed publication of reports that there was a link between thalidomide and peripheral neuritis.

In November the same year, William McBride, a young Australian obstetrician and gynaecologist with a large practice, noticed that the number of women giving birth to babies with defects was larger than would normally be expected, even in a practice many times the size of his. In looking for a common link, Dr McBride established that during their pregnancies, the women who had given birth to imperfect babies had all been prescribed Distavan by their GPs. This was the name by which thalidomide was marketed in Australia, by a subsidiary of UK's Distiller's Company Limited (DCL) – the company that made some of the most famous and popular brands of whisky, gin and other spirits

McBride's observations were confirmed by Widikund Lenz, a German research chemist. His tests showed that taken in the first three months of pregnancy, thalidomide could be responsible for phocomelia – a condition whereby babies are born with their normal limbs replaced by flipper-like appendages – and the drug was withdrawn. All anyone could do was sit, wait and see how many deformed babies would be born with defects caused by the drug.

Within a year of Dr McBride drawing the world's attention to thalidomide and the dangers it presented, 2,6000 thalidomide babies had been born in Germany, 400 in Britain, 39 in Australia and eight in New Zealand. The drug was withdrawn in most countries, apart from Japan. There, it continued to be sold over the counter even after its terrible effects were known, and as a result Japan had 1,000 thalidomide babies. Had the drug been withdrawn immediately its tragic side effects were know by the Japanese, the country would have had many fewer cases.

When Dr McBride's letter was published, the Australian manufacturer wrote to its parent company, DCL, in Britain. The letter eventually found its way to John Flawn, the export manager responsible for distribution to Australia. When he read it, he was horrified, not just because his company stood accused of marketing a dangerous drug, but because when he recalled the name under which thalidomide was marketed in Britain, he realized that his pregnant wife had taken it during her current pregnancy.

When the baby, later christened Alexander, was eventually born, it was horribly deformed – one of the worst of the UK thalidomide babies. He had one short, misshapen arm, the hand on which had no thumb, while his other hand had six fingers. His face was paralyzed down one side, one ear was missing, the other one was badly formed. If that wasn't bad enough, he had been born with brain damage, was deaf and dumb and was only partially sighted.

As more and more 'thalidomide' babies were

born, it became evident that the drug was one of the most teratogenic drugs that have ever been made. (The word means liable to produce malformed offspring from the Greek 'teratos' meaning monster and the verb-stem 'gen' meaning to produce or give birth to.)

The effects varied from baby to baby. Alexander Flawn was one of the most extreme cases. Others were luckier, being born perhaps with a missing finger or a malformed wrist. Between the two extremes, there were babies born with some or all of their limbs missing, there were children with no legs or arms but with their hands and feet appended to their shoulders or groins. Others were born with flipper-like limbs where their arms and legs should have been – phocomelia.

Babies were born blind. Some had no necks. Some had no or only partly formed genitalia. There were cases where surgeons had to create anal openings to allow faeces to be expelled from the body, babies having been born with the incomplete defaecatory apparatuses.

There were harrowing tales of mothers descending into clinical depression that lasted for years, when they saw the deformed babies they had just given birth to. One woman confessed to trying to suffocate her baby, only changing her mind and removing the pillow from its face when she saw the malformed little child – her child – struggle for life in its cot.

No one knows how many babies were born dead, their internal organs incapable of sustaining life, as a result of their mothers have taken the drug in all innocence, it having been, also innocently, prescribed by their doctors.

One country that escaped almost unscathed from the thalidomide scourge was the United States. With a population of over 180 million at the time, had the same proportion of thalidomide babies been born there as in Germany or the United Kingdom, there would have been around 10,000 deformed children in the US, if the drug been as widely prescribed there as in other countries. As it turned out, there were only sixteen thalidomide cases in the US. And the reason there were so few is largely due to one woman, Dr Francis Kelsey.

All countries have their own rules and regulations regarding new drugs. In the United States at the beginning of the 1960s the rules that were applied to drugs whose manufacturers sought the approval that was necessary before they could marketed were among the most stringent in the world. (Since the thalidomide case, these rules have been tightened up all around the world.)

With such a large population, the United States was an obvious and potentially profitable place for Chemie Grunenthal to market its new sleeping pill. But the first two companies that were offered the US marketing rights, Smith, Kline and French, and Lederie both turned it down. It was not until 1958, a year after thalidomide had first gone on sale in Europe, that the company found a taker – Richardson-Merrill.

Chemie Grunenthal gave Richardson-Merill the results of all their research, including the tests on cats and dogs, which had showed that in exceedingly high doses the drug could be lethal. Understandably, this was of little concern to the

American company, which spent more than a year investigating its new purchase. During that time, as part of its clinical trials, it distributed over two million tablets to more than one thousand doctors throughout the States. The doctors prescribed it to over 20,000 patients, none of whom suffered any serious side effects.

Confident that the federal Food and Drug Administration, the agency without whose authority new drugs cannot be sold in the United States, would approve the new drug, Richardson-Merill wrote, asking for its permission to launch thalidomide on the US market. It was to be sold there under the brand name Kevadon, and the proposed launch date was 6 March, 1961. Along with the application, Richardson-Merill sent details of all their tests and research.

The application landed on the desk of Dr Francis Kelsey, a 46-year-old woman who was new to the FDA and whose first case it was. Dr Kelsey was married to a chemist who helped her assess the information the company had supplied. The judgement was damning: "…an interesting collection of meaningless, pseudo-scientific jargon apparently intended to impress chemically unsophisticated readers', and 'the data are completely meaningless as presented' are just two of the phrased that peppered Francis Kelsey's report.

Her suspicions that the information the company had supplied was incomplete were aroused when she read a report in the British Medical Journal, commenting on the suspected link between thalidomide and peripheral neuritis. She was sure that this was something of which Richardson-Merrill must have been aware but of which there was no mention in their application for FDA approval.

Her reprimand to the company incensed executives there. 'The burden of proof that the drug is safe ...lies with the applicant,' she wrote. 'In this connection we are much concerned that apparently evidence with respect to the occurrence of peripheral neuritis in England was known to you but not forthrightly described in your application.'

Threatening litigation, the company went to the head of the FDA who asked Dr Kelsey to explain herself. But she was not a woman to be overawed by that. Prompted by the BMJ article, she said that she now wanted additional tests to establish if thalidomide was safe for pregnant women.

When the FDA bosses backed her, Richardson-Merrill had no alternative but to do what was asked of them. But before the company could submit a revised application, the fact that thalidomide was teratogenic began to emerge. Grunenthal was forced to withdraw the drug from the German market and advised all the pharmaceutical companies to which it had granted manufacturing and marketing licenses to do the same.

For saving the United States from the tragedy of thalidomide, Francis Kelsey was awarded a gold medal by President Kennedy. And as it turned out, Richardson-Merrill had reason to be grateful to her, too. When it was eventually forced to compensate the handful of American thalidomide victims, the company paid out several million dollars. Had the drug been widely available in the US and had the same proportion of thalidomide babies been born there as in Germany, it is estimated that Richardson-Merrill would have had to pay out over $5 billion.

In Germany, the case came to the attention of the public prosecutor's officer in Aachen. After several years of investigation, it was decided that there were ground to bring criminal charges against Chemie Grunenthal. Four years later nine of the company's executives were charged with intent to commit bodily harm and involuntary manslaughter. After another four years, hearings were suspended but the company was forced to hand over all of its profits to German thalidomide victims for ten years.

In Sweden, the parents of 105 thalidomide children took joint action against Astra, the company that has marketed the drug there. The company settled out of court and agreed to pay grants to the victims for the rest of their lives. The cost to Astra, should they all live to be 75, was estimated at $14 million.

In Britain, the story of the victims' struggle for compensation became almost as big as the story of thalidomide itself. DCL at first denied that it was responsible for the terrible side effects caused by the drug, which it had marketed under the name Distaval. DCL was backed by Enoch Powell, the Minister of Health in the Tory government of the day. In a written reply to the mother of a thalidomide baby born in Bristol, one of the Ministry's civil servants said that there had been no reason to suspect that thalidomide could have had the side effects it had. And, the letter pointed out, when the side effects presented themselves, the company had immediately withdrawn it from the market.

At first, the press accepted this, agreeing that DCL had acted honourably. But things were to change when the parents of 20 thalidomide children who were being cared for at Chailey Heritage, a sheltered workshop with access to the famous prosthetic limb centre at Roehampton in South West London, decided to take action. On learning that DCL was denying all responsibility and any negligence they took counsel's advice. When the parents were informed that a claim for damages for injuries sustained by a foetus was unlikely to succeed as in the eyes of the law the unborn child had no legal rights, they formed the Society for the Aid of Thalidomide Children. In Scotland, a similar association, the Kevin Club, was formed, named for a victim of the drug.

In 1962, the parents issued a writ against DCL. In doing so, they were unable to seek any public support because the writ made the matter *sub judice*, and therefore the press were unable to comment on it until the matter came to court.

The wheels of the law in such cases grind slowly, and it was not until six years had passed that DCL offered to settle with the parents of babies born after the link between the drug and peripheral neuritis had been pointed out to Chemie Grunenthal – 62 of the 420 children. But in agreeing to settle with those children, the company was denying all responsibility for children whose mothers took the drug before any adverse side effects were known.

While some parents were willing to accept the settlement, one man refused. David Mason was the father of a badly deformed thalidomide baby girl who, immediately after she had been born, had been taken to the Chailey Heritage where she would receive the professional nursing and upbringing she would need. The son of a DCL shareholder, it seemed to Mason that the company was putting shareholders' interests before those of the babies who had been born deformed because of a drug it had marketed.

In 1971, DCL offered to set up a trust fund of £3.5 million for the children and to give each set of parents £1,500. Each family would receive, on average, £8,000. The offer was conditional. It had to be accepted unanimously, by all the families involved.

Mason and his wife, Vickie, refused, and in December that year, told his story to *The Daily Mail*. Even as he was talking to the paper, investigative journalists from the *Sunday Times* 'Insight' team were looking into the story of the financial hardship being suffered by families of thalidomide children. In September 1972, their first report was published in the paper under the banner headline, 'Our Thalidomide Children: A Cause for National Shame.'

No one ever said, or even hinted that the company had ever tried to cover its involvement in marketing thalidomide in the UK and in some other areas of the world via its subsidiaries.

Nor has the accusation that it had deliberately tried to

mislead the Department of Health ever been laid at its door. But the charge that it had a moral responsibility was one that was to stick

Within a few days of the Insight team's feature being published, £35 million had been wiped of DCL stock market value. Shareholders began to put pressure on the board to increase its offer to the drug's victims and their families. At least one supermarket chain announced a total boycott on all DCL products, and the company was fast attaining pariah status in some sections of the press.

In the United States, Ralph Nader, the champion of American consumers and thorn in the flesh of many corporations and the US government wrote to the company, urging it to accept moral responsibility for all UK victims of the drug and to establish a £60 million trust fund. By his readings of the company's balance sheets, it could well afford to. And without actually threatening to organize a US boycott of DCL liquors, he hinted that if the company did not act generously and that if such a boycott did happen, there would be a big dent in the company's profits.

The British government was unwilling to become actively involved, but Jack Ashley, the member of parliament who so often championed the rights of the disabled, brought the matter to the attention of the House of Commons. In doing so he was backed by Barbara Castle, herself a doughty fighter for the underdog.

DCL offered to increase the trust fund it intended to establish to £5 million. David Mason, who was in Washington meeting with Ralph Nader, was incensed by the offer. To the anger of several of the other parents who were anxious to settle, but unable to do so with the approval of all the others, he refused. His daughter, Louse, was subject to the torment of some of the other children at the Chailey Heritage, when they heard that because of her father's refusal, they were forced to wait to see if they were ever to be compensated for their deformities.

It was not until 1974, that DCL increased its offer, promising to pay £2 million a year for ten years into the Thalidomide Trust. Barbara Castle, by now Minister of Health in Harold Wilson's cabinet, announced that the government would contribute £5 million by way of compensation against income tax.

The battle for compensation for the UK victims of thalidomide was finally over, thirteen years after Chemie Grunenthal had paid the equivalent of £150 to a minister whose nerve damage had been caused by the drug.

The story of thalidomide is not just a tragedy that need never have happened. There are many inspiring stories of victims of the drug triumphing over the adversity of their deformities: of girls with neither arms or legs growing up to have babies of their own: of young men and women unable to walk who have built up successful businesses. But perhaps best of all, of people for whom life was once thought hopeless living ordinary lives, holding down ordinary jobs, despite their deformities.

And the drug itself?

In 1998, in the United States, the FDA gave approval for thalidomide to be marketed for the treatment of erythema nodosum leprosum (ENL) a complication of leprosy that disfigures the skin, causing loss of feeling and that can, if not treated, lead to paralysis.

This type of leprosy affects only a few thousand people in the US, but now that the drug is approved, doctors can legally prescribe it for more people with other conditions. According to a recent survey, two-thirds of women in the US of child-bearing age are not familiar with the story of thalidomide. Because the drug might become available to women capable of having children, these women have to be warned about the serious risks of birth defects if the tragedy of the 1950s and 60s is not to be repeated.

1960

NEW YORK

Encore! Encore!

At the end of Puccini's opera, *Tosca*, the eponymous heroine, having just witnessed her lover, Cavaradossi, being shot by a firing squad, throws herself off the battlements of the Castel Sant'Angelo. Usually, she lands on a mattress, picks herself up and, after the curtain has fallen, makes her way back on stage to take her (usually but not always) well-deserved curtain calls. The audience who had sat enraptured through the opera at New York's City Center one night in 1960 had an unexpected bonus when a stagehand put down not a mattress but a trampoline. The great moment came! The rather large, American soprano playing Tosca cried out her final words – 'Scarpia, davanti a Dio' – and jumped. Only to appear again . . . and again . . and again. . .Fifteen times in all did the unfortunate woman bounce off the trampoline back into the audience's view – sometimes upside down, sometimes the right way up, screaming with rage. Such was her indignity that she felt unable to appear in New York ever again.

1961

NEW YORK

The wrong way of looking at things

For more than a month, the *cognoscenti* of New York flocked to the Museum of Modern Art to admire Henri Matisse's *Le Bateau*. The painting that measures 1420 x 1120mm (56 x 44in) is considered a masterpiece of 'Fauve' art. It was only after the painting had been on the wall for 47 days that someone noticed what none of the experts had spotted. Le Bateau had been hung upside down.

1961

SAN FRANCISCO

Following their lieder

Tosca again – this time in San Francisco. The opera is a favourite with many directors as there are only three principals – a chorus that appears in the first act, a shepherd and a choir in the second act, both singing offstage, a non-singing execution squad that appear in the third act and some other soldiers who run on stage just before the curtain comes down. On this fateful night, the last night of the season, the budget-conscious director recruited a group of enthusiastic young men from a local college to form the firing squad.

Unfortunately when every time they asked the harassed director, who was working to a tight schedule, when they should come on and what they should do, he brushed them off, saying that he was busy with the principals and would give them their instructions later.

Sadly for them, later never came. The dress rehearsal was cancelled for a variety of reasons and it was only a few minutes before the curtain went up that the boys in the squad eventually got their instructions. 'Right, boys,' he said, when you get your cue, slow march in, wait until the guy with the sword lowers it then shoot.' And when they asked how they got off, the producer told them exit with the principals.

Unfamiliar with the plot, which involves Tosca being tricked by the evil Scarpia into believing that the firing squad would fire blanks at her lover and that they would be allowed to leave Rome in secrecy, the boys marched on stage and saw not one principal as they had expected, but two.

The firing squad pointed their rifles at the man who, as he is in on the plot, pretends to ready himself for death while, at the same time casting sidelong, conspiratorial glances at Tosca.

Picking up the wrong signal, the boys turned and aimed their guns at the woman, who did her best via a series of negative gestures to get them to point their guns at Cavaradossi.

Now thoroughly confused, the squad had no idea who to shoot. Both, maybe? But if that was the case, why were they standing so far apart. Sombre funereal music was coming from the orchestra pit: they know the opera was called Tosca, and that it was a tragedy, so presumably the woman must die in the end, and there was something about the guy that suggested he expected to see the opera out.

That's why, when the officer in charge lowered his

sword, they shot Tosca. Imagine their astonishment, therefore, when she stood where she was and the fat guy slumped to the floor.

The only person who left the stage was the officer in charge, and as he hadn't sung a note, he was obviously not a principal and the firing squad stood their ground. They watched as Tosca rushed over to Cavaradossi and, thinking he was still alive, tried to rouse him and follow her into exile. Then realizing that she had been duped, and just as non-singing troops rushed on stage, Tosca ran to the battlements and readied herself to jump.

She was the only major character left on stage, and remembering the director's words to exit with the principals, when she jumped, the whole firing squad followed her.

1962

NEW YORK

The wrong arm of the law

The NYPD made a big mistake when they arrested small-time gangster Domingo Osario for driving the getaway car after a contract killing. They had to release the accused when Osario's lawyer pointed out that his client had no arms.

1963

NAIROBI

A ducal gaffe

The Duke of Edinburgh has, to put it bluntly, put his foot in it more than once. His injudicious remarks made during visit to China almost caused a diplomatic row. But he had no idea when he made a witty aside to the president of the country he was visiting in 1963 that his words would be broadcast quite so loudly.

It was during the Kenyan Independence celebrations at which he was representing the Queen. The ceremony had reached the point when, the speeches over, the Union Flag was about to be lowered for the last time and the new Kenyan flag hoisted in its place. It was just then that the duke turned to President Jomo Kenyatta and said, 'Are you sure you want to go through with this.'

Unfortunately, the microphones on the rostrum were still switched on and his voice boomed loudly on the ears of everyone present.

The Duke of Edinburgh: *open mouth, insert foot*

1965

LONG BEACH, CALIFORNIA

Looking danger in the eye

James Elliot was a wrong 'un. Even as a child it was obvious he was destined for a life of crime, and sure enough he was in and out of jail having committed a variety of crimes as soon as he reached the age of criminal responsibility. He eventually turned to armed robbery and one day in 1965 was holding someone up at gunpoint when his .38 calibre revolver failed to fire. Not being the brightest of men, and as his victim made good his escape, Elliot peered down the barrel to see what was blocking it, and pulled the trigger. Second time lucky!

1965

NEW YORK

Service with a smile

The staff at New York's exclusive Waldorf Astoria Hotel are well known for their polite manners and extremely helpful attitude to their guests. But they made the mistake of being over helpful to one guest who they saw tripping as he came down the main staircase one day in 1965. As he stumbled, the unfortunate man's suitcase dropped from his grasp and split open. Two bellboys sprang forward and helped the obviously stunned man repack the contents of the case, which, they noticed, included some rather good jewellery. The guest thanked them profusely before picking up his case, making his way across the lobby and into a cab, hailed for him by an obliging doorman. Later that evening one of the hotel's guests reported the theft from her room of half a million dollars worth of jewels.

1966

BERWICK-UPON-TWEED

Peace at last

The town of Berwick straddles the river Tweed, which forms part of the border between Scotland and England. For centuries it changed hands between Scotland and England, until, in 1482, it became part of England and has remained so ever since.

Berwick-upon-Tweed: *at war with Russia all by itself*

Although the two countries were united first in 1603 with the accession of James VI of Scotland to the English throne on the death of Queen Elizabeth I, and again in 1707 with the union of the two countries' parliaments, the town enjoyed a unique status. By convention, it was always referred to as a separate entity in all state documents and that tradition continued after the Union of the Parliaments.

Consequently, in 1853, when the Crimean War broke out between Russia and Britain, France and Turkey, the official declaration was made in the name of Victoria, Queen of Great Britain, Ireland, Berwick-upon-Tweed and all the British Dominions.

The war was won in 1856 and in Paris, after hostilities ceased, the peace treaty was signed by the British representative on behalf of Victoria, Queen of Britain, Ireland and all the British Dominions. No mention of Berwick-upon-Tweed: technically, the town remained at war with Russia – and did so until 1966.

In that year, 90 years after the treaty had been signed, an official from the Russian embassy visited the town to confirm that the war that had existed for so long between one of the world's two superpowers and the small English town was at last over. Peace was formally declared.

In acknowledging the historic event, Berwick's mayor, Robert Knox, thanked the Russian emissary and bid him to, 'tell the Russian people that at last they can sleep peacefully in their beds'.

1966

TEXAS

The worst driver in the world

In October 1966 in the small Texan town of McKinney, a 75-year-old driver was seen by the police to be driving on the wrong side of the road four times, causing six accidents, four of them hit-and-run, and as a result collecting ten traffic tickets. Not just in the space of one day, but all in the space of 20 minutes.

1966

MONTPELIER

When you've got to go

French ballerina Zizi Jeanmaire was one of the most glamorous of classical dancers the most stylish of women. Like most dancers she has made her fair share of mistakes, but the one she probably remembers the best is the night when she was on stage at the opera house in Paris when she realized that she had a pressing need to go to lavatory. She managed to hold on until her next exit but knew that she had no time to get back to her dressing room or to get to any of the lavatories before her next entry.

Desperate, she headed for the nearest wash hand basin, rearranged the costume she was wearing and clambered onto the sink, which promptly came off the wall, crashed onto the floor – and broke her foot.

1968

MARYLAND

Making the most of it

When 32-year-old Craig Boyden, who worked for a carpet company in Elliot City, Maryland, was diagnosed as having Crohn's disease he was naturally devastated. The disease, which affects the lower part of the bowel is incurable, and although those who suffer from it can, and usually do, live with the condition, in Boyden's case it was deemed by his doctor to be so far advanced that he had only three months to live.

Deciding to make the most of his last few weeks, Boyden embezzled $30,000 from his employers and went on a spending spree. He ate in the best restaurants in town, stood round after round of drinks to friends and acquaintances and threw a couple of lavish parties at his apartment.

As the weeks turned into months, Craig started to feel better . . . and better . . . and better . . . and decided that perhaps he should seek a second opinion. And that's when he learned that his doctors had made a mistaken diagnosis and he had made the mistake of not having their diagnosis confirmed before he embezzled the money. It transpired that he wasn't suffering from Crohn's disease after all, but from a simple hernia. The mistaken diagnosis had been caused by an allergic reaction to the gloves the surgeon had worn during exploratory.

Boyden's crime was detected a few days afterwards, but fortunately for him the judge saw the funny side of the story and gave him a suspended sentence, ordering him to repay the money he had stolen at the rate of $100 a week.

1969

BRAZIL

What Mama says, goes.

Would-be boxing champion, seventeen-year-old Manuel Salgado made a big mistake when he ignored his mother's warning about going into the ring – and suffered the embarrassing consequences. A few minutes into his first bout, the formidable Brazilian mama squeezed under the ropes and dragged Manuel away from his opponent, ordering the blushing bruiser to go home and finish his homework!

1969

TENNESSEE

Making his mark

When the burglar sizing up a house in Chattanooga one night in 1969, realized that he had left his gloves behind, he hit on the bright idea of taking his shoes and socks off and putting his socks over his hands. Police suspected that he was the culprit and took him in for questioning. The footprints he left at the scene of the crime proved to be the evidence the police needed to bring him to trial!

1970

WORCESTERSHIRE, ENGLAND

A catalogue of mistakes

In the days when cigarette smoking was more acceptable than it is today, several companies encouraged smokers to switch brands by putting collectable coupons in each packet. These could be exchanged for 'gifts' – each one costing a certain number of tokens. Joseph Begley from Malvern in Worcester duly saved 2,000 coupons and sent them off to be exchanged for a wristwatch. A few days later, he received a golf-bag, two electric blankets, a pressure cooker, some vinyl long-playing records, three tape-recorders, an assortment of pots and pans and not one but three of the watches he had ordered. Being an honest fellow, Mr Begley kept one of the watches, and returned everything else to the cigarette manufacturer.

A few days after that, he was delighted to receive 10,000 coupons from the company by way of thanks and apologies for being inconvenienced. Joseph looked at the catalogue that came with the coupons and selected some domestic appliances and a bedspread. A few days later a package arrived from the company – containing two stepladders and a plant stand!

Freebies: *tobacco companies and their incentives!*

1971

NEW YORK

Hand baggage!

Twenty-one year old Audley Gibson from Kingston in Jamaica was keen to travel to New York with his brother, but couldn't afford the fare. Not being especially tall and of slight build, the two young men suggested that Audley climb into the his brother's large, expanding suitcase. A few hours later, the suitcase was duly loaded onto the carousel at Kennedy Airport in New York. Passengers waiting to collect their baggage were horrified when one of the suitcases split open and a hand flopped out. Sadly, the Gibson brothers had overlooked the fact that the baggage holds in aircraft are unpressurized and Audley had probably died a few hundred kilometres into the flight, several thousand metres in the air above the Atlantic Ocean.

1974 -

LONDON

An intentional omission

In the early 1970s London publishers Weidenfeld and Nicholson commissioned Margery Fisher, one of the most respected names in the world of children's publishing to compile an A – Z of the best-known children's characters – *Who's Who in Children's Books.*

When the manuscript was received, the editor read it

through and realized that Ms Fisher had made a curious mistake. There was no mention of Enid Blyton's Noddy, surely one of the best-known characters of all in children's books.

Ms Fisher was contacted and the mistake was pointed out to her.

There was no mistake, said Ms Fisher. The omission was intentional.

The editor insisted – and that was her mistake, for when the short feature on the 'kind little fellow who lives in Toyland' was received, the second paragraph read as follows. 'This monotonously infantile character, who is frequently heard to say that he doesn't like being sensible but would far rather be silly, seems to have been put together from the weakest and least desirable attributes of childhood. It is hard to explain the persistent popularity of these trivial, repetitive stories with their small, retarded, masochistic hero.'

No mistaking Ms Fisher's opinion of Noddy!

Rejected: *no place for Noddy in the children's* Who's Who

1975

BERMUDA

Same time, same place!

More of a coincidence than a mistake, but worthy of note nonetheless. In Hamilton, Bermuda in 1975, a motor-scooter rider was knocked down by a taxi and died of his injuries. Exactly a year to the day earlier, the dead man's brother had been killed when he was knocked off his motor scooter, not only in the same street, by the same driver of the same taxi – with the same passenger in the back!

1975

ROTHESAY, SCOTLAND

Bungling bankrobbers

The three robbers who tried to hold up the Royal Bank of Scotland in 1975 made not one, but three mistakes. The first was getting stuck in the revolving door on the way in. They had to be freed by the staff. They returned unabashed a few minutes later and this time made it through the door only to be laughed at when they told the staff it was a holdup!

On hearing that no one was going to pay up, one of the gang made mistake number two when he vaulted over the counter and twisted his ankle. His partners in crime made mistake number three when they tried to make their getaway. They got stuck in the revolving door again.

1976

THE AMAZON

A fatal leap

When South American killer bees swarmed round a tourist from the United States as he stood on the banks of the Amazon, others in the group shouted at him to jump into the water. Sadly, he took their advice and took the plunge. Big mistake! He was eaten by voracious piranha fish.

1977

COUNTY DURHAM, ENGLAND

The wrong dating game.

It wasn't the jewel in their collection of coins, but the Roman *sesterce* from the second century AD has lain in its display case for several years in a museum not far from Newcastle in north-east England and had been much admired by thousands of visitors. But it was quickly removed by the embarrassed curator when a nine-year old budding numismatologist pointed out that the coin had been incorrectly labelled. It should have read, 'Promotional plastic token given away by a well-known soft-drinks company, c. 1970.'

1972

GUAM

The last man home

On 26 January, 1972, the following report appeared in *The Times*:

A Japanese soldier who remained faithful to his order never to surrender was captured yesterday after 28 years of hiding.

Sergeant Shoichi Yokoi, now 56, was surprised at nightfall by two hunters in the heavily forested Talofo River district 20 miles from Agana, while on his way to the river to set a trap for fish. They covered him with their rifles and marched him to a police station.

When he was found, Yokoi was heavily bearded and wearing clothes made from tree and bark fibre. He told his 'captors' that he had been working as a tailor when conscripted into the Japanese

Captured: *a Japanese prisoner is guarded*

army in 1941.

He had been posted to Guam, in the Pacific Ocean, in 1943 and when the Americans retook the island in 1944, he and two comrades had fled into the jungle, taking as many supplies with them as they could cram into their kit bags. Later, they learned from leaflets dropped from US planes and helicopters that the war was over in Guam, but not that the Japanese had surrendered in 1945 after atomic bombs had been dropped on Hiroshima and Nagasaki.

Fearful that they might be executed if they surrendered (and mindful of their orders never to do so), Yokoi and his two comrades dug a hole in the bamboo thicket and stayed there for several months until the food ran out. Then the others moved to another part of the forest, leaving Yokoi to fend for himself. They kept in contact, though, visiting each other occasionally, taking whatever food they had managed to hunt or trap. But one day after about eight years when Yokoi had gone to see his friends, he found that they had died of starvation.

Having burned his uniform on order, Yokoi had used a pair of scissors he had taken with him when he had reported for duty to shape the clothes he made for himself and to cut his hair. Apart from the scissors, the only relics he had kept from his army days were a waistband that his mother had embroidered for him, and a Japanese flag, both of which he had hidden in his cave.

Apart from the times he went to check on how his two former comrades were faring, he had stayed close to the cave at all times, rarely going out except at night and always staying in the same area.

He was examined by doctors who declared that apart from being slightly anaemic as a result of his salt-free diet, he was in excellent health. He was flown back to Japan, where he was told that as well as a pension of 10.00 Yen (£12.50 a month) he was entitled to back pay and allowances amounting to 43.131 Yen (£54)

When asked what he would like to do, he replied (as if having been alone in the jungle of Guam for well over twenty years was not enough) that he wanted to go up a mountain and meditate!

Schoichi Yokoi wasn't the last Japanese soldier to come home! In 1974, having survived in the jungle on the Philippine island of Lubang for 28 years Lieutenant Hiroo Onoda, surrendered his rusty samurai sword to President Marcos.

Unlike Schoichi who mistakenly believed that the war was still going on, Onoda had known it was over. But when he graduated from the Japanese Army Intelligence School in 1944, he had been given specific orders: 'To continue carrying out your mission even after the Japanese Army surrenders, no matter what happens.' When the island was liberated by American and Philippine troops, Onoda had gone into hiding with three compatriots. One had surrendered and two had died in shootouts with Philippine soldiers and policemen. Onoda had fought on for 29 years in all – unquestioningly following his rather outdated orders!

1976

EDGBASTON

A cricket balls up

It may not read like a mistake, until one realizes that the way the name 'Willey' is pronounced it rhymes with 'silly'. And that was the cause of one of the most hilarious incidents in the history of sports commentating.

During 1976 England v West Indies test match millions of listeners tuned into the match heard Brian Johnson make his now legendary gaffe. The words had hardly been spoken before there was a snort of laughter from Johnson's fellow commentator, who had just realized how Johnson's words must have sounded. For several minutes neither man was able to speak, as the sound of their helpless giggles was broadcast to listening cricket fans.

And the words?

'The bowler's Holding, the batsman's Willey.'

1977

TENERIFE

A plane crash – on the ground

Sunday is always a busy day at Tenerife's Santa Cruz airport with sometimes almost 200 planes taking off and landing, packed with holiday-makers either heading for the island's beaches or on their way home having enjoyed their vacations.

This particular Sunday was no exception, in fact it was busier than usual. A bomb planted by members of the Canary Islands Liberation Movement had exploded in a shop at Las Palmas airport on neighbouring Gran Canaria, resulting in flights being diverted from there to Santa Cruz. Among the diverted planes were two Boeing 747 Jumbo Jets. One, KLM flight 4805, from Amsterdam: the other Pan Am flight 1736 from Los Angeles and New York.

Flight conditions were far from ideal thanks to thick cloud and fog banked up around Pico de Teide, Tenerife's extinct volcano. By early afternoon, Santa Cruz was overcrowded with eleven planes on the ground, most of them awaiting clearance for take-off. The three air-traffic controllers on duty were becoming more and more harassed as the fog thickened and then an electrical fault put the central runway's lights out of order. And as if that wasn't bad enough, two of the airport's three radio frequencies went out of action, which resulted in all the pilots having to talk to the controllers via the one that was still working, shouting to make themselves heard through the babble.

On the Pan Am Flight, tempers were starting to rise. The 370 passengers had each paid $2,000 for a cruise that was scheduled to sail from Las Palmas. Their liner was ready and waiting when news of the bomb had come through and the pilot had been ordered to divert. They had been kept on the tarmac for two hours, unable to disembark because there weren't enough landing steps to service all the planes! The captain Victor Grubbs did his best to alleviate his passengers' boredom as they waited to finish their flight by asking them up to the cockpit in groups.

Meanwhile, on board the KLM jet the captain, Jaap van Zanten, realized that when they eventually got to Las Palmas there would be a long line of planes in the refuelling queue. So rather than face another lengthy delay there, he decided to fill his tanks at Santa Cruz with enough fuel for the short hop to Gran Canaria and the flight back to Amsterdam.

With visibility down to around 500 metres and the fog thickening even more, both captains were getting anxious. Neither wanted to have to tell their already fretful passengers that they would have to spend the night at Santa Cruz. Both wanted to get to Gran Canaria as soon as possible.

Just after 5.00pm word came from the control tower for both captains to prepare for take off. The main runway at the airport, which is about 650 metres above sea level, is 3.2 kilometres long, running from east to west. It runs parallel to a second runway used for taxiing to and from the terminal buildings. Four access slipways along their lengths link the two runways, which loop together at the ends.

On this particular day, because of congestion on the second runway, both pilots were told to move their planes on to the main one. They arrived at the east end at around the same time and they were told by control to taxi to the take-off point at the far end. With the KLM jet in the lead, the two pilots followed instructions.

Fog was swirling around and with no ground radar the controllers were unable to follow the movement of slow-moving aircraft on the runway. They had to rely on the one, busy radio channel to keep in communication with van Zanten and Grubbs.

Shortly after the KLM pilot was told to 'taxi straight ahead to the end of the runway and make backtrack,' the Pan Am captain heard that he was to taxi forward and to leave the runway by turning into a slipway on the left. Victor Grubbs had a choice: he could have used either slipways C3 or C4. Taking C3, which leads straight back to the terminal building, would have involved a 130-degree turn – a cumbersome manoeuvre for a plane as large as a 747. C4 leads in a circle to the top of the runway, where Jaap van Zanten was swinging his plane round in readiness for take-off.

Just as the Pan Am plane was passing C3 and heading for C4, the KLM co-pilot was on the radio, telling the controllers that 'Flight 4805 was ready for take off. We are waiting for clearance.'

The reply, 'OK. Stand by for take-off. I will call you.'

came back immediately.

Next, the tower asked the Pan Am 747 if it had cleared the runway. When told that it had not, the co-pilot was asked to report immediately the runway was clear. But moments later the KLM plane began to move – the two planes, one trundling along at a snail's pace, the other thundering towards it at 240km/h, were on collision course.

Through the fog the co-pilot of the Pan Am plane saw lights ahead. At first he thought it was the KLM plane standing at the end of the runway. But then he realized they were coming towards him. 'Get off! Get off!' he screamed, 'we're on the runway! We're on the runway!' as the pilot desperately put his plane into a 30-degree turn to get it out of the way of the approaching Jumbo.

There was no way that the KLM plane could stop. Moments before it smashed into the American jet, van Zanten lifted the nose, obviously in a desperate attempt to jump his plane over the other one. A blink of an eye later, the KLM's nose hit the top of the Pan Am, shearing off the roof of

Grounded: *few survived the Tenerife air disaster*

the cockpit and the first class compartment. Then, the Dutch plane's engine pods hit the American Boeing, instantly killing most of the passengers on the aft-cabin.

Unaware of what had happened, the air traffic controllers told a Spanish plane that was asking for permission to land to wait, until they had contacted the KLM pilot. But the Dutch plane, its tanks full of fuel, had turned into a fireball as it slewed up the runway. Suddenly, a gust of wind cleared the fog for long enough for the controllers to see the mobile inferno. A moment later, there was another gap in the fog and the Pan Am was seen, flames leaping from it high into the air.

Everyone on board the Dutch plane was killed. They included a woman who had told her husband that she was going to Spain for a holiday and not that she was flying to the Canary Islands with one of his best friends. Also on board was a Dutch businessman who had boarded with a neighbour with whom he had been having an affair. He had told his wife that he was flying to Switzerland on business. Before he left, he wrote a loving post card to his wife and gave it to a colleague to post in Zurich. Two days after the plane crashed, the card was delivered to her.

Surprisingly, a few people sitting up front or on the left-hand side of the Pan Am plane managed to scramble to safety. One woman, who was pushed through a hole in the fuselage by her husband, and then dragged her mother to safety, later recalled seeing some passengers sitting strapped to their seats, too traumatised to make any attempt to free themselves. They, and more than 300 other people died on the Pan Am Boeing.

582 people perished in that plane crash, more than had or have died in any plane crash before or since. All such accidents are tragic: the fact that both planes were on the runway makes the mistakes that caused the Tenerife air disaster all the more poignant.

1978

TORTOSA, SPAIN

A tragic refusal to listen

For months, locals who lived near the campsite at Los Alfaques close to the town of Tortosa in southern Spain had been complaining to the authorities that tanker drivers were using the dangerous, twisting coast road rather than pay the toll on the nearby expressway. Residents were alarmed, for they knew the trucks were full of pressurised liquid gas from the refinery at Tarragona, between Barcelona and Valencia.

The authorities made a fatal mistake when they refused to listen. In July, 1978, the wished they had. It was then that a tanker crashed through the campsite wall and burst into flames. Blazing gas spewed over a 400-metre radius and a 60-metre ball of fire swept through the site, setting caravans and tents ablaze. The force of the explosion was so strong that holidaymakers were blown across the sandy beach into the sea.

More than 170 men, woman and children died, many of their bodies little more than blackened, unidentifiable stumps: and all because a driver refused to pay 1,000 pesetas (around £7.00) to take the safe road.

1978

WASHINGTON DC

She was not amused

It was the night of the year for many in Washington's diplomatic community – the president's annual diplomatic reception, with guests from all the embassies dressed in all their finery. It was an evening for black tie and tails, tiaras and tittle-tattle.

The food was superb, the wine was fine: too fine for one of President Carter's brightest and most respected aides. After drinking one glass too many, his tie loose and the top button of his shirt undone, he sauntered across to the wife of the Egyptian ambassador and making as if he was about to lower the bodice of her frock said, 'I've always wanted to see the pyramids.'

History does not record if he had drunk so much that he suffered a memory loss when he awakened the next morning. It didn't really matter if he did for there was a report on his gaffe, splashed across the newspapers for the entire world to read. They also recorded the fact that shortly after he had upset the lady, he announced to her that he was 'going for a pee!'

1979

LOCH BUDHIE, SCOTLAND

The little loch

When the members of a Cornish scuba-diving club decided to go to Scotland to dive there, they pored over the maps before deciding that Loch Budhie would be ideal. And being a law-abiding group of men and women, they contacted the loch's owner well in advance to get his permission. When the local laird wrote to the divers, giving the go-ahead one can't help but wonder if he had a smile on his face as he sealed the envelope. Because after a journey of over 1,100 kilometres and after heaving their heavy equipment 1,000 metres up a mountain to reach the loch, the scuba-istas were disappointed to find that the loch was just fifteen centimetres deep!

1972

LONDON

The wrong day to do it

The plan was simple. The drugs being smuggled into the country would be dropped overboard in the Thames estuary, to be picked up by one of the gang who stole a barge in which to make the rendezvous. Unfortunately, the gang chose a day when there was dock strike. As theirs was the only craft on the move in that part of the Thames, the suspicions of the river police were quickly aroused. Arrests followed with equal rapidity!

1979

HOLLYWOOD

Crossed lines

When Hollywood legend Mae West was in her 80th year, she agreed to appear in a film, *Sextette*, directed by Ken Hughes. Miss West had come to stardom when a script was a script: once she had learned it, that was it – no changes. She was unused therefore to the modern practice of rewrites, often on the hoof, and found herself unable to keep up with the pace of change, having learned her lines only to find them changed, then changed again.

Hughes came up with a solution. Miss West agreed to have a small radio receiver fitted to her wig and her lines were delivered to her by the director, moments before she was due to speak them.

The other actors found it a bit disconcerting, hearing Hughes' voice coming from Ms West's wig, often reacting to lines that had still to be spoken. But they put up with it, until by accident, a police traffic helicopter tuned into the same wavelength as the actress's receiver during a torrid love scene. No one present will ever forget the moment when Mae West responded to a whispered word of love during a passionate embrace with the immortal line: 'Traffic on the Hollywood Freeway is bogged down!'

Mae West: *come up and see me sometime, traffic permitting*

1980 – BRADFORD

A casebook of mistakes

For five years, women around Bradford were constantly on the alert in case the 'Ripper' struck again. But in 1980, Peter Sutcliffe was found guilty of 13 charges of murder and was sentenced to life imprisonment.

Twelve years later, he confessed to an attack for which he had not been charged. On 27 August, 1975 he had beaten a fourteen-year-old girl, Tracy Browne, about the head with a hammer in a lane at Silsden, to the north-west of Bradford. After the assault he had then thrown her over a fence and made his way home. But thanks to the full moon that had been shining, Tracey had seen her assailant quite clearly and was able to give the police a detailed description of him. When the ID picture, showing a man with short dark hair, a beard and a gap between his front teeth was printed in local newspapers in West Yorkshire, Peter Sutcliffe turned to his mother-in-law and joked that it could have been him.

Two years later, when the Ripper was front page news not just in Yorkshire's three ridings but all over the country, Tracy told the police that she was convinced that she had been attacked by him. They dismissed her story. Had they listened to her several young women would probably still be alive today. They didn't.

Peter Sutcliffe was born in a small mill town, Bingley, nine kilometres north of Bradford. A shy boy, he was regarded as a bit of weed at school where he was frequently bullied. When he was fifteen, he got a job as a gravedigger at Bingley Cemetery. It was here, he was to tell police years later, that he heard the voice of God telling him to go out into the streets and kill prostitutes.

In 1969, he attacked for the first time, hitting a Bradford prostitute over the head with a heavy stone when arguing over her £10 fee for services rendered. The woman survived.

So, too, did the next two women he attacked. In July 1975 when he was in Keighley, he attacked a woman called Anna Rogulskyj with a hammer. He was just about to finish her off with a stab wound to the stomach when he was disturbed by a passer-by. A week or two later, he struck again when he rained a succession of vicious hammer blows on Olive Smelt, a Halifax office cleaner. Only when he was caught in the headlights of an approaching car, did Sutcliffe run off.

On 30 October 1975, a Leeds milkman, delivering in Chapeltown, the city's red light district, found the battered body of Wilma McCann. A post mortem showed that she had been bludgeoned from behind with a hammer and her clothes had been torn from her body. After she had died, her body was stabbed fourteen times in the chest and stomach.

Three months later, Sutcliffe killed again in Chapeltown. This time his victim was 42-year-old Emily Jackson, her clothes, like

McCann's, ripped from her to leave her breasts exposed. She had stab wounds on her chest and there was a footprint on her right thigh: a size seven Wellington boot, a small size for a man.

Part-time Chapeltown prostitute Irene Richardson was the third woman Sutcliffe killed, in February 1977, but in the meantime he had savagely attacked another prostitute, Marcella Claxton, in Leeds. After having 50 stitches put in her head, Claxton told police that her attacker had black hair and a crinkly beard.

After the post-mortem on Richardson, the police knew that the same man was responsible for the three killings, all of which bore the same trademarks – multiple fractures of the skull, clothing ripped off to reveal the upper chest and stab wounds on the breasts and lower abdomen caused by either a knife or a screwdriver.

120 detectives were assigned to the Richardson case. In an attempt to trap the killer, policewomen disguised as prostitutes walked the Chapeltown streets. Nothing happened, other than that the police became more and more bogged down with checking and cross-checking statements. Even before the task was just beginning, Sutcliffe struck again, in April 1977. His victim was yet another prostitute, Tina Atkinson, whose body was found at her flat on the fringes of Chapeltown. The police hardly needed to examine the body to tell it was the work of the same killer –the size-seven Wellington bootprint on a bedsheet told them that.

Sutcliffe, by now having been given the sobriquet 'The Yorkshire Ripper' struck again in June 1977. This time his victim was sixteen-year-old Jayne MacDonald. Astonishingly, until now, no single officer had been put in overall charge of the investigation, but such was the outcry that followed Jayne's death that Yorkshire's chief-constable, Ronald Gregory, was forced to put his most experienced officer, George Oldfield, in charge of the investigation.

By this time, Sutcliffe had married his girlfriend of eight years, Sonia Szurma, a schoolteacher. For the first three years of their marriage they lived with her parents before moving into a house in Heaton, a middle-class Bradford suburb not far from the town's red-light district, which was centred on Lumb Lane.

For his next victim, the Ripper was back on familiar territory. Before she stepped into her client's brand new red Ford Corsair, Manchester prostitute Jean Jordan took £5 from him as an advance and then directed him to a patch of open land three or four kilometres from her Moss Side home – a popular spot for prostitutes and their clients. A few minutes later, Jordan had been bludgeoned to death. Sutcliffe had no sooner dragged her body into the bushes, than another car turned up, forcing him to leave with all possible haste. It was on his way back to Bradford that he realized that the note he had given Jordan was a brand new £5 from his wage packet and may, just possibly, be traceable back to him.

For several days he anxiously scanned the papers, looking for reports that the Ripper had struck again. When, after just over a week later, there was nothing, he decided to take the risk of returning to the scene of the crime to try to retrieve the incriminating evidence. When he could find no sign of her handbag, he started to try to disguise the hallmark signs that this was another Ripper killing. He found a piece of broken glass and began to attack Jordan's corpse: but the glass was not sharp enough to have much effect and, frustrated, he gave up and drove back to Bradford.

Jordan's body was found the next day and not far from it, the police uncovered her handbag and in it the £5 note. It was traced back to a bank in Shipley where Sutcliffe was now working as a driver for a haulage company who were one of the bank's customers. Everyone on the company's payroll was interviewed, including Sutcliffe, who was visited twice by policemen. Both times, the officers left the Sutcliffe household with no reason to believe that they had just spoken to the killer.

As part of the investigation, the police were interviewing motorists whose cars were regularly spotted in the Bradford and Leeds red-light districts. When it was noted that Sutcliffe's red Corsair had been seen in Lumb Lane on seven separate occasions, police officers again called on him at home. Sutcliffe explained that Lumb Lane lay on one of the routes on which he occasionally drove home. After verifying that Lumb Lane was on her husband's way home from work, Sonia Sutcliffe dismissed out of hand any suggestion that her husband had any reason to use prostitutes.

To be fair to the police, a vast amount of paperwork was generated by the case. But the fact that ten months after he had been interviewed about the £5 note found in Jean Jordan's handbag no one spotted that there was something to else to link Peter Sutcliffe with the Yorkshire Ripper is surprising – some might say astonishing.

Among the countless other pieces of paper that were part of the investigation were two letters that had been received the previous year. Written by the same hand (something that was verified by experts) and both bearing Sunderland postmarks, the letters had both been signed 'Jack the Ripper'

In March 1979, by which time the Ripper had killed three more times, he claimed his ninth victim, Vera Millard, who he murdered in the grounds of Manchester Royal Infirmary where she was a patient. The police concluded that the murderer could only have known this if Millard had told him and that the letter must indeed have come from the Ripper. A full-investigation was launched in Sunderland, which yielded no new leads but added more to the already vast mountain of paperwork.

Eleven days after the letter was received the Ripper struck again. This time his victim was a building society worker, Josephine Whitaker.

On 18 June, 1979 a package was delivered to Assistant Chief Constable George Oldfield. Written in a hand now familiar to the policeman, the envelope contained a cassette tape. 'I'm Jack,' the voice said, 'I see you are having no luck catching me. I have the greatest respect for you, George, but Lord, you are no nearer catching me now that you were four years ago when I started. I reckon your boys are letting you down, George. They can't be much good can they?'

The voice that echoed round the office where the cassette was played had a pronounced Geordie accent. After listening to it again and again and again, dialect experts said that the speaker came from Castletown, a small mining community in Tyne and Wearside.

So convinced were the police that the voice was the Ripper's, instructions were issued to everyone working on the case that anyone who did not have a Geordie accent could be eliminated from the enquiries.

A month after the package was received by the police, officers were back at Sutcliffe's house once again – this time because his car (now a Sunbeam Rapier) had been seen in Lumb Lane no fewer than 36 times. The detectives interviewing Sutcliffe had no idea that he had been interviewed before, so out of date was their paperwork. But there was something about Sutcliffe that rang an alarm bell in the mind of one of the interviewing officers, Detective Constable Andrew Laptew.

Sutcliffe's height and build, his collar-length, black hair, his beard and Saddam-Hussein style moustache and the gap between his front teeth all matched the scanty descriptions that the women who had escaped from the Ripper at the beginning of his murderous spree had given. Not just that, he had small feet and was a lorry driver – the Ripper's suspected occupation. When he got back to his office Laptew checked through the records and found that in 1969, Sutcliffe had been arrested for 'going equipped to steal.'

All this Laptew put in a

two-page report but it lay unread for nine months. When it did come to the top of the enormous pile, because neither Sutcliffe's voice nor handwriting matched the Geordie tape and letters, it was filed. A month after Laptew had interviewed Sutcliffe, the Ripper had killed his eleventh victim, Barbara Leach.

Having interviewed more than 150,000 people, checked 15,000 vehicles, taken 22,000 statements and spent £3 million, the police were becoming more and more convinced that the best clue they had was Jean Jordan's £5 note and that the killer was one of the 8,000 men interviewed in that connection.

Had they fed all these names into a computer along with the names of the owners of the vehicles that had been seen in the red-light districts often enough to arouse suspicion, and run a cross check then the name Peter Sutcliffe would surely have come up. But they didn't, preferring instead to rely on an outdated card-index system.

As they painstakingly went about their investigation, news came through that voice experts at Leeds University contradicted previous opinions about the tape and that it was a hoax. Some of the officers working on the case were not surprised: none of the women who had escaped the Ripper had mentioned a Wearside accent, indeed one had been quite definite that he spoken with a local Yorkshire accent.

Some of the policemen had also realized that there was nothing in the letters that could not have been gleaned from the newspapers. Even the connection between

Manchester Royal Infirmary and Vera Millward on which Oldfield had put so much importance, had been reported in the *Daily Mail*.

These misgivings were passed up to the top, but were ignored. Despite what the experts at Leeds University had said, the Chief Constable of West Yorkshire was convinced the tape was genuine. He arranged to have it played on radio stations and at soccer matches across Tyne and Wearside, hoping that someone would recognize the voice. 50,000 people thought they did.

By the beginning of 1980, the police had narrowed down the number of firms who could have issued Jean Jordan's £5 note to three companies – one of them T. and W. H, Clark (Holdings) Ltd of Shipley – the haulage company for which Sutcliffe worked.

On January 13, when police were in Shipley making preliminary inquiries on this lead, Sutcliffe jumped down from the cab of his lorry to be interviewed by them. He was wearing the same Wellington boots that the police had a sole print of

Pig in a blanket: *the Ripper has his day in court*

– the ones found close to the bodies of two of the Ripper's victims. No one noticed.

Two days later, he was questioned again as part of the screening of all the company's employees. His clothes were scrutinized carefully and Sonia Sutcliffe was questioned about his movements on specific days over the past few years. They also asked her if he had any sexual deviations or a taste for unusual sexual practices. If he did, Mrs Sutcliffe didn't tell the police about them, and they left the house obviously satisfied.

On 2 February, Sutcliffe was one of the Clarke drivers who were asked to take a handwriting test. Apparently he was shaking like a leaf and sweating profusely when he was taken to the station, but as the official line remained – the cassette and letters were genuine – and as Sutcliffe spoke with a West Yorkshire accent and his handwriting didn't match that on the letters, he was released.

In June that year, Sutcliffe was breathalyzed when he was caught speeding through Bradford's red light district. He was cleared, but there must have been something about his manner or attitude that aroused the suspicion of the two policemen for they suggested to the Ripper squad that they take a look at him. They were told that he had already been seen and had been eliminated from inquiries.

Getting more and more desperate and with the press and public becoming increasingly agitated about the their failure to make any progress, the police decided (in the words of Mrs Thatcher *apropos* the IRA) to starve the Ripper of publicity. Sutcliffe knew that his twelfth victim, in August 1980, was Marguerite Walls.

But the killing received little coverage in the press and was not suspected as being the work of the Ripper. Similarly, when a Singapore doctor, Upadhya Bandara, was attacked in Headingley but left alive as the assailant was disturbed before he could kill her, it was described as a random attack.

Peter Sutcliffe killed for the thirteenth time in November 1980. This time his victim was young student – Jacqueline Hill. In the catalogue of mistakes that seems to have been the hallmark of the police investigation into the case of the Yorkshire Ripper, their handling of the murder of Jacqueline Hill stands out.

When a fellow undergraduate found a handbag on the pavement, less than 400 metres from where Dr Bandara had been attacked, and noticed several spots of blood, the police were called. Inside the bag there was a cheque guarantee card, embossed with the name 'Jacqueline Hill'. When the student who called the police suggested that it might be a good idea to find out where Ms Hill lived and see if she was alright, they treated her like an adult might when confronted with a cocky child.

Their cursory search of the area failed to reveal the pair of broken glasses or woollen mittens that were lying close to where the bag had been found. But most extraordinary of all, they missed Jacqueline Hill's body, which was lying less than 30 metres from them. They took the bag back to the station where it was registered in the Lost Property book.

When the body was found, it was clear to everyone,

including the public, that the Ripper had struck again. Among the information that the police gave to the press was that a brown car had been spotted near the scene of the crime. The description of it was so similar to a new Rover Sutcliffe had bought that it prompted Trevor Birdsall, a man whom Sutcliffe regarded as a friend, to write to the police anonymously:

'I have good reason to know [sic] the man you are looking for in the Ripper case. The man as [sic] dealings with prostitutes and always had a thing about them. His name and address is Peter Sutcliffe, 6 Garden Lane, Heaton, Bradford. Workes [sic] for Clarks [sic] Transport, Shipley.'

If Birdsall expected the police to act quickly, he was disappointed. So when he had heard nothing about Sutcliffe being arrested, he went to the police station accompanied by his girlfriend where he repeated what he had written. He also told the police officers who took his statement that he had been with Sutcliffe in Halifax on the evening of 16 August, 1975, the night when Olive Smelt had been attacked (Smelt was the girl whose life had been saved by approaching car headlights as the Ripper made to finish her off, had been attacked). Sutcliffe, according to Birdsall, had got out of his car to go after a woman that night.

Trevor Birdsall was thanked politely for taking the time to come in and tell the police what he had – and heard nothing more from them!

By the end of 1980, George Oldfield who had suffered a heart attack eighteen months before probably brought on by the pressure he was under and who had missed many crucial months of the investigation, was dropped from the case. In his place, Chief Constable Gregory replaced him with Oldfield's deputy, Jim Hobson, at the head of a think-tank of senior officers drawn from forces from all over the United Kingdom.

Two days into the new year, two policemen patrolling Melbourne Avenue in Sheffield's red-light district, saw a woman, Olivia Reavers, get into a Rover V8 and went to investigate. When asked what his name was, the driver identified himself as Peter Williams. When he asked if he could go and relieve himself, the police had no objection. He moved into a dark alley out of sight from the police and was back a few seconds later, still pulling his zipper up. When he got back to the car, he found the woman he had picked up arguing with the police about her loss of earnings. As she berated one of the officers, the other one was checking the car's number plates and found out they were false. Williams was taken in for questioning.

At the station, 'Williams' told the police that he was really Peter Sutcliffe. He thought he was being questioned about a traffic offence, but he was unaware that Ronald Gregory had ordered that when anyone the slightest bit suspicious was picked up in any red-light area in his territory, the Ripper Squad were to be alerted. Sutcliffe was taken to Dewsbury police station where he was questioned by Detective Sergeant Desmond O'Boyle. Sutcliffe made no secret of the fact that he had been questioned several times during the Ripper inquiry.

After several hours

questioning, O'Boyle could find no reason to hold Sutcliffe any longer and was about to let him go when his chief superintendent told him to persist. Sutcliffe agreed to give the police a blood sample – he had little option; to have refused would have aroused suspicion even more.

Back in Sheffield, when Detective Sergeant Robert Ring the policeman who had arrested 'Peter Williams' earlier heard that he was still being questioned in Dewsbury in association with the Ripper case, he decided to do a little investigating of his own. He returned to Melbourne Avenue where, close to the spot where 'Williams' had gone to urinate he found a hammer and knife. It later turned out that Sutcliffe had taken them out of his car coat pocket and hidden them behind a clump of bushes in the alley.

Back in Dewsbury, the results of the blood test came through. Sutcliffe was blood group B, one shared by only six per cent of the population. That and the weapons Ring had found were enough to tell the police that they had their man.

When presented with the evidence Sutcliffe confessed.

He pleaded not guilty to murder on the grounds of diminished responsibility. But the jury preferred to believe that he was a cold, calculating evil killer rather than an insane one and returned to the court with a guilty verdict. The judge sentenced him to life imprisonment.

Given that the police had had an accurate description of what the Ripper looked like since 1977: given that they had the computer technology to cross reference all their inquiries in a fraction of the time that it takes using a card index: given that they were told in August 1979 that the Geordie accent was fake, but that they continued to believe that the cassette was genuine: given that Sutcliffe was interviewed at least eight times before he was picked up in Sheffield's Melbourne Street – given all that, it is small wonder that the Ripper Inquiry has gone down as one of the most bungled murder hunts in recent times.

1981

SWINDON, WILTSHIRE

The right number

The burglar who broke into a large house in the Gloucestershire side of Swindon while the owner was sleeping had the cheek to call his accomplice on the household telephone and say he was ready to be picked up. Unfortunately, the driver didn't get to the phone on time, but suspecting it was his partner in crime, he made the mistake of dialling the caller's identity number to call whoever had just called him – waking the owner who promptly called the police!

1984

LOS ANGELES

'Not one of our smarter robbers.'

54-year-old Charlie Murphy went into his local Safeway one day in June 1984 and filled out an application form for a store credit card. He put down his real name, his social security number and his address before handing the card in. The real intention of his visit had not been to apply for credit but to case the joint. Less than half and hour later he was back. He went to the same window and demanded money from the cashier, saying he had a gun in his pocket. At the last minute his nerve failed him and he ran off, empty handed.

It didn't take the manager long to recall that the would-be robber and the card-applicant were one and the same person. No sooner had he got to his apartment than the police were knocking on his door. As one of them said later, 'he was not really one of our smarter robbers.'

1985

OKLAHOMA CITY

A confession – of sorts

At the trial of Dennis Newton on a charge of armed robbery, the defence were quietly confident. The main witness had given stuttering testimony against their client, while he had handled himself admirably in the witness box. But sadly for them, when the supervisor of the store that had been held up was asked by the District Attorney if she could identify the culprit, and she did so very hesitatingly, the defendant jumped to his feet and shouted, 'I should have blown your head off when I had the chance!' Case proven.

1987

SOUTHERN ENGLAND

Stormy weather

On 15 October there was a depression starting to develop in the Bay of Biscay as warm air over Africa moved north and confronted cold air from the Arctic air mass. Where the two masses met, a frontal system developed, with the warm air being forced to rise above the cold, creating a drop in air pressure.

At around 18.00, the depression suddenly

deepened, probably as a result of interaction between a strong jet stream – air from Hurricane Floyd, which was moving up the east coast of the USA and across the Atlantic – and exceptional warming over the Bay of Biscay. As a result of this, large quantities of water vapour condensed to cloud providing an enormous release of latent heat energy. In layman's terms, a storm was brewing.

It was predicted that it

Big wind: *the unexpected hurricane that struck England in 1987*

would track along the English Channel. However the depression veered north catching the men in the meteorological office by surprise. The storm tracked along the north coast of Cornwall and Devon, across central southern midlands to the Wash, with the strongest winds being recorded in the south-easterly quadrant of the storm, crossing the English side of the Channel and moving through Hampshire, Sussex, Surrey and Kent.

Half an hour after midnight, ships in the shipping areas Thames, Dover, Wight and Portland were warned of severe gale conditions. An hour later, police and emergency services were alerted to expect severe weather. At 05.30, the weather centre at Heathrow Airport recorded that the wind was blowing at 94km/h. Later, in London, the reached 150km/h – above hurricane force.

Millions of people who watched the weather forecast after the BBC Nine o'clock News, which had warned of gale force winds of 50km/h, probably thought that a few tiles may be loosened, the odd branch blown from a tree or two. When those who had managed to sleep through the hurricane awoke the next morning, the scenes that met their eyes were among the worst that have been seen.

Felled trees were blocking roads and railway lines. Houses and buildings all over the area had their roofs blown off. On the Isle of White, the Shanklin Pier, one of the island's most famous landmarks, was reduced to a pile of driftwood. In Essex, the Jaywick caravan park was flattened. In Folkestone, a ferry was blown aground and its crew had to be rescued.

Fifteen million trees were uprooted, including one third of those in London's Kew Gardens. In some woods in the Home Counties, hardly a tree was left standing.

Hundreds of thousands of homes were without power for over 24 hours.

Insurance claims ran into billions of pounds. In the London Borough of Ealing alone, 600 people called their insurance companies regarding damage to their cars.

Sixteen people lost their lives. The toll would have been much higher had the storm hit during the day. As it was, most people were in their beds and the roads and streets were quiet. Had it been rush hour, there would have been hundreds, maybe thousands of accidents.

Experts said that it was the worst storm to have hit England since 1709. It was, they claimed, a 'once in 300 years event'. They were wrong. Another storm, admittedly not quite as severe as the 1987 hurricane, swept across southern England just 27 months later.

One man who will never forget the 1987 Hurricane is BBC weatherman Michael Fish. When he was warning the nation of strong winds, he said, 'a lady has rung in to ask if there's going to be a hurricane tonight. There is not.'

Technically he was correct. He had been asked about a tropical cyclone in the west Atlantic. But in not making that absolutely clear, he will forever be the man who got it wrong!

1989

SHEFFIELD

A tragic mistake

It should have been a great sporting occasion. The semi-final of the FA Cup at Hillsborough, in Sheffield, neutral territory for the two teams – Liverpool and Nottingham Forest – competing for a place in the finals.

It was a beautiful late spring day. The gates had opened at 12.00, three hours before the kick-off and the atmosphere was good natured as the crowd streamed in through the turnstiles. The police knew that thousands of fans were travelling from Liverpool and Nottingham to cheer on their teams. But from a crowd-control point of view things seemed to be going smoothly until around 14.30 when a crush developed at the two Lepping Lane entrances– the end where the many of the Liverpool fans had been allocated tickets.

Delays on the motorways, at coach parks and railway stations had resulted in many fans arriving much later than they had anticipated and rushing to get to their places before the three o'clock kick off.

As more and more people arrived, the police tried to close perimeter gates to relieve pressure at the turnstiles, but this only seemed to make matters worse, and so the gates were opened again at around 14.50. Minutes later 2,000 fans had moved through the gate, walking briskly, most heading straight down a tunnel which led at a one-in-six gradient to an already tightly packed pen.

The gradient and the momentum led to a domino effect with thousands losing their footing and becoming unable to control their momentum or the direction in which they were being pushed. With more and more people coming through the tunnel, pressure on those at the front of the pen became unbearable.

At 2.54 the teams came onto the pitch. Fans at the back, unaware of what was happening at the front, pushed forward to get a better view, intensifying the already terrible pressure. People at the front, fearful of being crushed to death, started to clamber over the barrier. With the teams already on the field, and the authorities believing that unruly crowds were causing a disturbance, the police tried to push people back over the barriers.

It wasn't until 15.06 with the game underway that a policeman realized what was happening and the referee was ordered to stop the game.

But it was too late for the 96 fans – men, woman and children – who had been crushed to death because of the mistakes that had been made.

The mistake of closing perimeter gates then reopening them again.

The mistake of not learning from a previous overcrowding incident at the same ground in 1981 when Spurs fans had been packed into the same part of the stadium.

The mistake of not postponing the kick-off for a few minutes to allow the crowd to get into the stadium safely.

The mistake it was later revealed of letting police review and alter their written recollections of the event.

Eleven years after the tragedy, the two, by then retired, senior policemen who had been on duty that day were tried for manslaughter in a private prosecution brought by the relatives of those who died. The six-week trial ended with one of the men being found not guilty and the jury being unable to reach a decision regarding the second. The judge ordered that there should be no retrial. In the eyes of many, another in the catalogue of mistakes that combined to cause the Hillsborough Disaster.

1990

SOMEWHERE IN SPACE

A billion-dollar booboo

In the 1980s, NASA authorized the building of a space telescope to be put in orbit around the Earth. Its mission was to take photographs of the far reaches of outer space and to transmit them back to scientists. Such a telescope, they hoped, would eliminate the effects of irregular air movements, atmospheric dusts and gases, light pollution and the other factors that distort earth-bound telescopes, many of which are built high up in remote places to reduce distortions.

It was decided to dedicate the project to Edwin Hubble (1889 – 1953) an American astronomer who had first noted the paradox that the more distant a galaxy was from the Earth, the more rapidly it was receding into space. Sometimes called 'the red shift' this had led to the conclusion that the universe was still expanding, which in turn led to the 'Big Bang' theory of the creation of the universe, an event that is now estimated to have happened some fifteen billion years ago.

With an estimated cost of $1.5 billion, the Hubble Telescope is the most expensive scientific instrument ever made. And with such a vast sum involved, the American taxpayers who were funding the project could have been forgiven for believing the men from NASA would have got it right . . .

Work got underway, and by 1988 the telescope had undergone test after test after test. A few flaws were discovered and the planned launch date was postponed. Over the next few months, several major components were removed, repaired and reinstalled, and on 25 April, 1990, by now long behind schedule, the crew of the US space shuttle *Discovery* put the telescope into orbit.

Almost from the very start, things started to go wrong. While the Hubble was being deployed, one of its two solar-powered, generating panels refused to open properly. But just as two of

Houston, we have a problem: *control centre for the Hubble space telescope*

Discovery's astronauts were getting ready for an unscheduled space walk to pull it out manually, the panel did as had been planned, and opened up of its own accord. Then, a malfunctioning cable obstructed one of the telescope's antenna. But that was soon put right and the Hubble began to do the job it had been designed to do.

Back on Earth, scientists sat in front of their screens, to see images of whatever the Hubble had in its sights – and with $1.5 billion spent on the project, they had every right to expect that these would be crystal clear and sharper than anything yet seen. It's not hard, therefore, to imagine their disappointment what they saw was no better than the images supplied by terrestrial telescopes.

It wasn't long before the reason became clear: a mistake had been made during the optical testing stage, resulting in the images being affected by a spherical aberration that exaggerated any natural blurring by a factor of ten.

The investigation revealed that one of the parabolic reflectors had been ground to the wrong shape – and the mistake had been made when the project was in its infancy. In 1981. When the optics had been assembled and tested, one of the lenses used in the testing had been out by 1.3 millimetres. This had been caused by scientists misinterpreting the position of an image produced by an aperture at the end of one of the measuring rods. 1.3 millimetres might not seem much, but when working to a degree of accuracy of less than one thousandth of a millimetre, the image would be distorted by a factor of over 1,300 – something that would make a dried pea about the size of a Rolls Royce!

Computers were used to enhance the images being sent back by the Hubble and the results were of such a high standard that the blushes eventually receded. But the telescope's troubles were still not at an end and at the end of 1993, an elaborate and needless to say expensive mission had to be mounted to effect repairs to the Hubble. A space shuttle was positioned alongside the telescope and a special crane was used to take it aboard. There part of the lens system was replaced that corrected the original mistake made during testing twelve years before. At the same time, some of the electronics were renewed along with some of the instruments, and two of the solar panels were replaced. Investigation revealed that some of the casings were found to be disintegrating.

The Hubble Telescope is now fully operational and has sent back some breathtaking images from space. The birth of new stars and the death of old ones, asteroids and comets, the creation of new galaxies and many more previously unseen wonders of the worlds out there have all come in the telescope's ken.

But thanks to the mistakes made at the beginning, the Hubble Telescope cost more than half-a-billion dollars more than was budgeted for the project.

1993

LIVERPOOL

'And they're off . . .'

The Grand National is, perhaps, the most famous and gruelling race in the steeplechase calendar: twice round the famous Aintree race course – and twice over the infamous Beecher's Brook, perhaps the most famous fence in the steeplechase world. It has been the scene of some memorable events. There was 1956 when the Queen Mother's horse, Devon Loch, with Dick Francis in the saddle was comfortably in the lead. The finishing post was twenty metres away when Devon Loch slipped, lost his stride and stumbled to the ground, powerless as ESB caught up, overtook him and won the race. There was 1967 when eleven horses were either brought down or balked at the 23rd fence. Suddenly, through the melee, galloped Foinavon, so unfancied at 100-1 that neither her owner nor trainer had bothered to attend. And then there was 1993 . . .

The horses lined up at the tapes, but one of them, Royal Speedmaster, was causing so much trouble that the starter, Colonel John White, had no alternative but to indicate to the jockeys that the start would be delayed for a moment. It was a chilly, drizzly day, and with the wind getting stronger and the excitement of the crowd near the starting line communicating itself to the horses, they were getting more and more nervous the longer the start of the race was delayed.

And they're off!: *or perhaps not...*

The horses were eventually recalled and were soon milling round the line, the jockeys trying to get them into some sort of line that would enable the starter to raise the tapes for 'the off.'

The horses on the inside were quick to get away, clearing the first fence then the second, Sure Metal in the lead. What they didn't realize was that when the Starter released the tapes, it did not go up quickly enough and caught round one of the horse's necks and then entwined itself around jockey Richard Dunwoody. The starter raised his flag to indicate a false start and to recall the runners, but the flag had not been unfurled and the race official down the track did not wave his flag to indicate to the jockeys that the race was going to have to be restarted.

The course commentator announced the false start across the PA system, but the shouts and the jeering of the crowd blanketed out the sound from the jockeys' ears.

As the horses approached The Canal Turn, the crowd were waving their hands in the air and some were booing, but with their minds on the race, the horses thundered on. Up the back they galloped and as they approached the Melling Road, the BBC commentator said to the millions of astonished viewers watching the fracas, 'Well here's one of the greatest sensations ever in the National. There are nine horses still at the start'.

The horses rounded the Home Turn and took the two fences before The Chair, one of the stiffest tests Aintree has to offer. An official there waved desperately at the horses as they roared past him, but the jockeys assumed they were being warned either of an obstacle or protestors, and that they were being waved to the left. That's where they headed and The Chair now behind them, galloped towards the water, by which time the group was now strung out.

As they approached the end of the first circuit, another official tried to wave them down. A few of the jockeys sensing something was up, perhaps realizing that the people milling around on the course were not protesting 'animal lovers', but race officials and fellow jockeys, reined their mounts in.

By the time the horses still left in 'the race' approached Beecher's for the second time, there was bedlam on the course. Horses that had taken no part in the race were milling around the start line. Horses that had completed one circuit were being detacked and rubbed down by anxious stablelads.

By now only seven horses were left in 'the race'. They skimmed over Valentine's and into the back straight where the leaders took the fences there in their stride. Crossing the Melling Road for the second time, they came into the straight. The three leading horses were neck and neck as they approached the last fence. Esha Ness took it much better than The Committee and Romany King and stormed towards the line to win the race that never was.

1995

STRATFORD-UPON-AVON

An untimely slip

Countless mistakes have, no doubt, been made on the stage of the Shakespeare Memorial Theatre at Stratford-upon-Avon – missed cues, late entries, dropped props, audiences have seen them all.

But the people at a performance of Romeo and Juliet one night in 1995 witnessed one of the funniest – for other members of the cast and the audience perhaps: not for the poor actor involved.

It was towards the end of the last act. Romeo had poisoned himself. Juliet had wakened from her drugged sleep, seen her dead lover and stabbed herself with a dagger. The stage was filling with the Duke and his entourage, various Montagus and Capulets and assorted townspeople. The audience were listening attentively to the closing speeches when one of the actors in the crowd stepped backwards – and fell off the stage.

Many actors have fallen off the stage. Most of those who have headed straight for the pass door and backstage. Not this young man. To the huge amusement of the audience he began to climb back on stage. Had he been tall and had the stage not been quite so high he might have done so quite quickly. But he was short and the stage was high above the stalls. For several minutes while the audience guffawed his fellow actors did their best to hide their giggles. But the harder the now perspiring actor tried to get back on stage, the louder the audience roared and the more the cast shook with paroxysms of silent laughter.

Eventually he made it. He took his position on stage. The laughter subsided and the actor whose line it was gulped hard when he remembered what he had to say. After taking deep breath Lord Capulet stepped forward and said, 'What should it be that they so shriek abroad?'

Collapse of audience and everyone on stage.

1997

LONDON

Wizard mistakes!

Many people make the mistake of thinking that they can write children's books – and make the even greater mistake of submitting their efforts to publishers' offices where, very often, unsolicited manuscripts can lie around for several months before it is eventually sent back with a polite rejection slip. But there are the odd occasions when it is not a would-be author who made the mistake of over-estimating her sales potential, but the several publishers who turned her manuscript down. One such case is that of the Edinburgh author whose manuscript was turned down by all the London-based publishers to whom it was submitted until it was submitted to one that made no mistake. The publisher? Bloomsbury Books! The author? J. K. Rowling. The book? *Harry Potter and the Philosopher's Stone*. It, and the ones that followed it made millions for Ms Rowling and boosted Bloomsbury's balance sheet to the sound of much gnashing of teeth in the children's divisions of other major publishers.

1998

LEWES, EAST SUSSEX

The case of the handcuffed juryman

After four weeks of hearing the evidence against a quartet of ne'er-do-wells accused of a jewel robbery in Brighton, the jury retired to consider their verdict. One of the exhibits in evidence was the pair of handcuffs with which the gang had planned to disable the jeweller, and the foreman of the jury asked that they be brought to the jury room so they could be inspected.

Unable to resist the temptation to see if they worked or not, the foreman slipped them over his wrists, clicked the lock and – Yes! They worked very efficiently. Unfortunately, no one had brought the key, so there was no way of freeing him. The judge called the fire brigade, but just before they arrived he remembered that no one apart from court officials was allowed to enter the jury room. Then the chief fireman told the judge that his sister-in-law was on the jury.

Eventually the judge ruled that the court be cleared and the jury recalled to the box. Only then was the trapped foreman freed from the bonds that bound him. And when the embarrassed man apologized for his mistake, the judge insisted that the mistake was his for not warning the jury about experimenting with the exhibits. ☼

2000

LONDON

A landmark mistake

One of the decisions that John Major's Conservative government took when it was in power during the mid-1990s was to mark the Millennium by building a splendid dome on a piece of land that bulges into the River Thames at Greenwich, in the east of London.

When the Tories were booted out in the New Labour landslide of 1997 the Blair government confirmed that the Dome would go ahead. It would, ministers said, become a landmark symbol of 'Cool Britannia' – the image of modern, trendy Britain with which they wanted to impress the rest of the world.

By the time the great and the good gathered in the dome on New Year's Eve 1999, the cost had doubled from £500 million to £1 billion. But not to worry, the public were told: people would flock to it, and the cost would be recouped in a few years.

The crowds stayed away in their droves and when it became obvious that far from covering its costs millions would have to be spent to subsidise the dome every year, New Labour stared losses in the face – and decided to cut them.

In 2002, the dome was sold off for a fraction of the money it had taken to build it, and as part of the complicated deal, the taxpayer continues to subsidise it to the cost of £250,000 a month.

To be fair, though, far from being the first or the only case where those who commission public works have made the mistake of believing that what was being built would be brought in within the estimated budget, the Dome is one among many.

When the Suez Canal was finally opened in 1869, the final cost was twenty times higher than the original estimate.

In Australia, the budget for the Sydney Opera House was A$7 million. The final cost of it was A$102m, almost fifteen times over estimate – and far from being the best opera house in the world, according to opera and music lovers it doesn't work terribly well. And in the United States, the Boston Big Dig cost $6 billion more than the estimated $8 billion.

Meanwhile back in Britain, the Humber Bridge cost £151 million, just over five times the allocated £28 million: while in Edinburgh, the budget for the new parliament building (at the time of writing still unfinished) has risen tenfold from the original £40 million. That figure pales into insignificance when compared to the £4.7 billion that the Channel Tunnel eventually cost – that's £2.1 billion more than was first thought.

In London, when developers decided to invest in the Barbican development which now dominates the skyline around St Paul's Cathedral, they thought that £8 million should cover it. At £187 million, the final cost was more than ten times the estimate. The Jubilee Extension Line designed to carry the millions (who never turned up) to and beyond the Dome, cost £1.4 billion more than the £2.1 billion the planners had estimated.

By comparison the final cost of the new British Library, between Euston and St Pancras Stations, seem paltry – a mere £511 million. The original estimate was £74 million. Some of the overspend in this particular case was caused by the usual delays, spiralling labour and material costs. But much of it was due to the fact that when quality control experts were called in to cast their eyes over the (they thought) almost finished building, they found 230,000 items that needed to be replaced or put right.

2002

LONDON

Poor Liza

Broadway and Hollywood star Liza Minnelli made a costly mistake when she thought the man waving to her from the pavement as her car was caught in the London traffic was a fan. She wound down the window, stuck her hand out to wave back and thank the man for his warm greeting. A few seconds later, the stunned Ms Minnelli slumped back in her seat as her 'fan' ran off to be lost in the crowds, carrying the £20,000 gold watch he had wrenched from her wrist.

2002
LONDON

A 'bloody' expensive mistake

Charles Saatchi, co-founder of one of the most successful advertising agencies of recent times, is also one of the most enterprising collectors of modern British art. His collection is perhaps the most comprehensive in Britain.

He is also the partner of kitchen 'goddess' Nigella Lawson. When they were moving into the house she was to share with Saatchi it is Ms Lawson who is said to have told one of the workman that she wanted the deep freeze compartment taken from where it was and where it was to go in the new kitchen.

No doubt assuming that the freezer had been emptied, the workman unplugged it and left it in position to be moved later. It was only when a thick, red liquid started to ooze from it, that they realized that there had still been something in the freezer when it had been switched off.

The 'something' was 'Self' – a blood sculpture by Marc Quinn, who had sprung to fame in the early 1990s with his provocative, conceptual works. 'Self' was certainly provocative: a representation of the artist's head, cast from several litres of his own blood.

There was nothing to be done. The sculpture had disintegrated so much that it was beyond repair – the £13,000 Saatchi is reputed to have paid for it melted before Ms Lawson's eyes.

2003

SOMERSET

The homing instinct

After a night on the tiles with a friend in Axbridge, a small town in England's West Country, Mark Norely, a 34-year-old scientist managed to get home. Once there, he went straight to his room and climbed into bed. The only trouble was that neither the house he had headed for nor the bed in which he slept were his. He had moved seven years earlier.